ASIAN
AMERICANS

CRITICAL PERSPECTIVES ON ASIAN PACIFIC AMERICAN SERIES

Critical Perspectives on Asian Pacific Americans aims to educate and inform readers regarding the Asian Pacific American experience and critically examines key social, economic, psychological, cultural, and political issues facing Asian Pacific Americans. The series presents books that are theoretically engaging, comparative, and multidisciplinary, and works that reflect the contemporary concerns that are of critical importance to understanding and empowering Asian Pacific Americans.

SERIES TITLES INCLUDE

Juanita Tamayo Lott   *Asian American: From Racial Category to Multiple Identities* (1997)

Diana Ting Liu Wu   *Asian Pacific Americans in the Workplace* (1997)

SUBMISSION GUIDELINES

Prospective authors of single or co-authored books and editors of anthologies should submit a letter of introduction, the manuscript or a four to ten page proposal, a book outline, and a curriculum vitae(s). Please send your book manuscript/proposal packet to:

Critical Perspectives on Asian Pacific Americans Series.
AltaMira Press
1630 North Main Street, Suite 367
Walnut Creek, CA 94596
(510) 938-7243

ASIAN AMERICANS

From Racial Category to Multiple Identities

Juanita Tamayo Lott

ALTAMIRA
PRESS

A Division of Sage Publications
Walnut Creek • London • New Delhi

For information:

AltaMira Press
A Division of Sage Publications
1630 North Main Street, Suite 367
Walnut Creek, CA 94596
explore@altamira.sagepub.com

SAGE Publications Ltd.
6 Bonhill Street
London EC2A 4PU
United Kingdom

SAGE Publications India Pvt. Ltd.
M-32 Market
Greater Kailash I
New Delhi 110 048 India

Printed in the United States of America

Library of Congress Cataloging-in-Publication Data

Lott, Juanita Tamayo.
    Asian Americans: from racial category to multiple identities / by Juanita Tamayo Lott.
        p.   cm. — (Critical perspectives on Asian Pacific Americans series)
    Includes bibliographical references and index
    ISBN 0-7619-9172-7 (cloth). — ISBN 0-7619-9173-5 (pbk.)
    1. Asian Americans—Race identity. 2. United States—Race relations. 3. Asian Americans—Statistics. I. Title. II. Series.
E184.O6L68   1998
305.895′073—dc21   98-8882

98 99 00 01 02 03 10 9 8 7 6 5 4 3 2 1

CONTENTS

CHAPTER THREE
CONTINUING UTILITY OF DIRECTIVE 15 49

CHAPTER FOUR
ASIAN AMERICANS: A RACIAL CATEGORY 69

CHAPTER FIVE

ABOUT THE AUTHOR

Juanita Tamayo Lott is a public policy consultant based in Silver Spring, Maryland.

ACKNOWLEDGMENT

The poem *What Are You?* is used with the permission of Joanne Nobuko Miyamoto. Reprinted from *Asian Women,* a publication by students at the University of California at Berkeley. Copyright 1971.

DEDICATION

This is dedicated to my parents, Lazaro Lorenzo Tamayo and Anicia Lucas Tamayo.

WHAT ARE YOU?

when I was young
kids used to ask me
what are you?
I'd tell them what my mom told me
I'm an American
chin, chin, Chinaman
you're a Jap!
flashing hot inside
I'd go home
my mom would say
don't worry
he who walks alone
walks faster

people kept asking me
what are you?
and I would always answer
I'm an American
they'd say
no, what nationality
I'm an American!
that's where I was born
flashing hot inside

and when I'd tell them what they wanted to know
Japanese
. . . Oh, I've been to Japan

I'd get it over with
me they could catalogue and file me
pigeon hole me

so they'd know just how
to think of me
priding themselves
they could guess the difference
between Japanese and Chinese

they had me wishing
I was American
just like them
they had me wishing I was what I'd
been seeing in movies and on TV
on bill boards and in magazines
and I tried

while they were making laws in California
against us owning land
we were trying to be american
and laws against us intermarrying with white people
we were trying to be american
our people volunteered to fight against
their own country
trying to be american
when they dropped the atom bomb
Hiroshima and Nagasaki
we were still trying

finally we made it
most of our parents
fiercely dedicated to give us
a good education
to give us everything they never had
we made it

now they use us as an example
to the blacks and browns
how we made it
how we overcame

but there was always
someone asking me
what are you?

Now I answer
I'm an Asian
and they say
why do you want to separate yourselves
now I say
I'm Japanese
and they say
don't you know this is the greatest country
in the world
Now I say in america
I'm part of the third world people
and they say
if you don't like it here
why don't you go back.

—Joanne Nobuko Miyamoto (1971: 50-51)

CHAPTER ONE

RACE: A MAJOR ORGANIZING PRINCIPLE

... blood, darky, Tar Baby, Kaffir, shine, moor, blackamoor, Jim Crow, spook ... quadroon meriney, redbone. high yellow ... Mammy, porch monkey, home, homeboy, George ... spear-chucker, schwarze, Leroy ... Smokey ... mouli, buck, Ethiopian, brother, sistah

—Trey Ellis
(as quoted in Gates, 1995: 424)

BACKGROUND

At the beginning of this century, sociologist W.E.B. Du Bois commented that the color lines would be the problem of the 20th century. Since then we have witnessed the civil rights movement and changes in immigration laws that together have resulted in a multiethnic and multiracial American society. On the eve of the 21st century, we find ourselves asking the question, "Does race matter?" This book addresses this difficult question by examining the experience of Asian Americans as a racial category and as a multiplicity of identities in the United States.

Today, Asian Americans are becoming a significant population. Demographically, they are the fastest growing racial/ethnic group. They doubled their population between 1960 and 1970, between 1970 and 1980, and again between 1980 and 1990. Economically, Asian Americans had the highest median household income of all households at $37,007 in 1990 (U.S. Bureau of the Census, 1993a: Table 3, 1993b:

15

Table 48). Politically, Asian Americans are wielding their clout at local and national levels. There are currently two Asian American governors—Filipino American Ben Cayetano, elected governor of Hawaii in 1994, and Chinese American Gary Locke, elected governor of Washington in 1996. On a global level, Asians are over half the world's population, comprising 3.5 billion of 5.8 billion persons in 1996 (Population Reference Bureau, 1996).

The social significance of Asian Americans is that they are neither White nor Black. Their prominence as a racial group is both similar to and different from other racial and ethnic minorities. They have been associated with Blacks and other racial/ethnic minorities as a member of historically disadvantaged groups in the United States. In the past, they had experiences of harsh discrimination similar to Blacks. In recent decades, they have come to be associated with Whites due to similar socioeconomic and educational attainments and similar residential patterns. Despite their being subject to discrimination, they have historically had much higher levels of intermarriage than Blacks. Some have been classified as "honorary" Whites. Asian Americans thus constitute a group for scrutiny in questioning the continuing salience of race and racial discrimination.

ORIGINS OF GROUP CLASSIFICATION IN THE UNITED STATES

The United States has selectively defined various groups since its founding. Historically, racial categories per se were not used to differentiate minority groups in the American population. Instead, groups of people were accorded a different civil status to distinguish them from the initial settlers who were of Western European origins. The only racial category was that of White. The Naturalization Act of 1790 limited citizenship to free White persons (males) who had resided in the United States for two years. Broad groups defined as not belonging to the White race included indigenous tribes, slaves from Africa, residents of Spanish America, and immigrants from southern Europe and Asia. These populations were initially excluded from becoming full citizens.[1]

Long before any sizable immigration of Asians to the United States, American public policies distinguished between Western European White settlers and others. Blacks and American Indians were defined not only by their lack of citizenship status but also by their relationship to the process of production. Takaki described this relationship in terms of the development and maintenance of an American capitalistic economy:

> The most important basis for these differences in racial attitudes was the relationship of each group to the process of production. Jefferson and the American economy has located them in different places. The black was a slave worker within white civilization and his labor was essential for white men like Jefferson to accumulate surplus, expand their capital, and also pay off their debts which some of them insisted, originated from the purchase of slaves. The Indian was not a laborer but an occupant of "vacant" lands which white men like Jefferson desired in order to expand their land holdings, as well as the national boundaries of white settlement, and to increase agricultural production. (Takaki, 1979: 64)

The civil and economic status of groups were the initial and primary basis for group classification. Other classifications included nativity (foreign born or American born), labor force participation (employed or unemployed), and socioeconomic status (wealthy or poor). These group classifications overlapped with racial and ethnic classifications to such degree that they often were used interchangeably.

Racial and ethnic categories have been used in the United States to distinguish groups in relation to a White majority. This differential treatment has been used for purposes of both exclusion and inclusion. A three-way racial classification was embedded in the first census of 1790 which identified Whites, American Indians, and slaves. Beginning with the first census, the United States government distinguished between American citizens who were free, White, adult male property owners and all others. As stated in Article 1, Section 2 of the Constitution,

> Representatives and direct Taxes shall be apportioned among the several States which may be included within this Union, according to their respective Numbers, which shall be determined by adding to the whole Number of free Persons, including those bound to Service for a Term of Years, and excluding Indians not taxed, three-fifths of all other Persons.

The 1790 census distinguished Indians, the indigenous residents of this land, for purposes of taxation but not representation. People of African ancestry were classified as slaves and were counted for apportionment purposes as three-fifths of a White person. During this time, Blacks composed 20 percent of the new nation. Not all Blacks were slaves. About one in ten was free at the time of the first census.

Throughout the 19th century, particularly after the Civil War, the Black population continued to be differentiated in greater detail by color, blood quantum, and free status. In subsequent censuses, attention was given to nationality and ethnicity-related items to inform immigration policies restricting immigrants from Southern, Central, and Eastern Europe and later from Mexico and Latin America.

The first policy of exclusion specifically directed at a national origin (rather than a civil or legal status), however, did not occur until late in the 19th century. It was not directed to Blacks nor American Indians but was directed to an Asian group. The 1882 Chinese Exclusion Act curtailed immigration from China. This was followed by the 1907 Gentlemen's Agreement between Japan and the United States, which limited the entry of Japanese immigrants.

Differentiation occurred regardless of the numbers of these populations. These other groups—including Blacks, American Indians,

Chinese, and Japanese— were enumerated separately over several censuses, even when they were a minuscule proportion of the total population. For example, in the 1930 census (one of the more detailed listings of racial and ethnic groups) Mexicans at 1.4 million comprised only one percent of the population. Indians at 332,954 were one-fifth of 1 percent (U.S. Department of Commerce, 1933: Table 4).

Classification in the early censuses was production based, racially preferential to property-owning White males, and was arbitrary in relation to population size. Overall, classifications reflected a class-stratified, racially hierarchical system of access to resources that was monitored by White men in power. Since citizenship, voting, and property ownership were tied to race, it became necessary to monitor the size, location, and growth of other populations.

Selective designation has not been limited to census data but is also found in other statistical systems. For example, until 1989 natality statistics on children with one White and one non-White parent designated the children as non-White. Where both parents were non-White, children were assigned the father's race, except in Hawaii where if either parent was Hawaiian, the children were designated Hawaiian (Hahn, 1992)

With Reconstruction and suffrage, there was a shift in the uses of classifications. Racial categories began to reflect the government's needs to ensure more equal access to resources by all groups. Since World War II, with the broad enactment of civil rights statutes, racial and ethnic data have been used to monitor discrimination against racial minority groups in various areas such as housing, education, employment, voting rights, and the justice system. The goal of civil rights statutes is to guarantee inclusion and full citizenship participation. Civil rights laws do not specify individual racial and ethnic groups but forbid discrimination on the basis of race, color, creed, or national origin. In the effective enforcement of such laws, however, racial and ethnic groups are classified and designated.

MINORITY GROUP CLASSIFICATION

For years, the study of race relations in the United States has been dominated by Black/White relations, with Indian/White relations mentioned parenthetically.

Blacks

Minority group status has been most affiliated with the Black population. For over 200 years, the United States has been described as a Black and White society with a White majority and a Black minority (Hacker, 1992). Blacks have been defined not as a people unto themselves but only in relationship to Whites. This relationship is one of power with Blacks as a minority subordinate group and Whites as a majority dominant group.

Population coverage in the decennial census was initially viewed in terms of free persons and slaves resulting in unequal representation for apportionment purposes. Despite the fact that at the time of the American Revolution ten percent of Blacks were free Blacks, free persons were synonymous with Whites and slaves were synonymous with Blacks (Farley and Allen, 1987: 9). As recently as the 1990 census, the most recognized measure of underrepresentation is in terms of the undercount of the Black population. The underclass continues to be most associated with a Black minority.

White Ethnics

A steady stream of immigration from Eastern Europe after the Civil War through the beginning of the 20th century brought a new population group into the United States—Eastern, Southern, and Central European immigrants who were initially distinguished from the Western European settlers as other races, such as Italian race or Polish race (Lieberson, 1980: 5). Eventually, these groups became part of the

American melting pot who could assimilate into a White America. They had access to public education and became part of the working and middle classes. They found opportunities for employment and upward mobility in a growing industrial economy. The first generation of Eastern European immigrants was viewed as a hyphenated American. Over time, however, as second and third generations were established, they were incorporated into a more inclusive White category. By contrast, later generations of non-White groups continued to be considered distinct.

Non-Black Minorities

Other people of color—whether indigenous to the Americas, non-White settlers with several generations of U.S.-born residents, or newly arrived immigrants and refugees—have been primarily defined as non-existent. When other people of color have been recognized, it has been in a marginal and stratified fashion. They have been defined not only in relation to a dominant White society but also in relation to a Black society defined by the federal government as the "principal minority" (Office of Management and Budget, 1978).

A Black and White view of race in the United States is in sharp contrast to the history of the Americas and to the emerging future of the United States as a multiracial society. Racial and ethnic diversity existed in the Americas long before the founding of the United States. Indigenous peoples from the Hawaiian Islands to the Caribbean and across North America were neither White nor Black. They were joined in the post-Columbian period by peoples of African and Spanish ancestry. This intermingling of indigenous peoples, explorers, colonizers and missionaries produced "mestizos," a uniquely New World mixture of African, European, Indian, and, with the Manila Galleon Trade, Asian ancestries.

Less commonly articulated is the minority group status of populations that are neither White nor Black. This is true of indigenous peoples, particularly among American Indian tribes which maintain legal relationships with the federal government (Snipp, 1989). With statehood, the minority group status of Aleuts and Eskimos in Alaska and Hawaiians in Hawaii has become prominent.

Hispanics, as a minority group, are both distinct from and similar to the above racial groups. They are the only recognized multiracial group in the sense that Hispanics may be of any race. There are, for example, White Hispanics and Black Hispanics. In the Southwest, a Hispanic presence dates back to Spanish America, giving Hispanics a residential status similar to American Indians. That is, Hispanics predate Whites in the United States. Like Asians, Hispanics also include new settlers, with steady immigration from Mexico and Latin America. Finally, despite European origins, the historical treatment of Hispanics being less than equal to Whites is similar to the treatment of Blacks (Bean and Tienda, 1987).

The minority group status of Asians is less visible nationally due to their historically fewer numbers, concentration in the West, and a perception that they are new settlers. The latter view is reinforced with continuing immigration from Asian countries over the past two decades. Their minority group status is traced to three historical instances of exclusion—anti-Asian immigration laws, Supreme Court naturalization rulings that reinforced Asian immigrants as aliens ineligible for citizenship, and the World War II internment of U.S. citizens of Japanese ancestry.

In short, race continues to be a major organizing principle in the United States for Black and non-Black minorities, including Asian Americans. *Race was originally used as a proxy for a civil status distinguishing citizenship and majority status.* Since then it has been treated as a basic demographic variable defining the American population. This has persisted despite political and socioeconomic gains of racial minority groups in the post World War II era and especially with the enforcement of civil rights statutes and policies.

GROWTH OF RACIAL-ETHNIC MINORITIES

While the intersection of demography and policy confirms the importance of race as an organizing principle, it also raises the general question, "Do racial and ethnic categories matter in an increasingly multiracial society?" This has become a particularly intriguing question as racial minority groups increase their proportion of the American population and improve their ranks in higher education and professional occupations.

The numbers of people of color are growing at a high rate across all regions of the United States. Between 1960 and 1990, due to relaxation of immigration restrictions and natural increase, the numbers of racial/ethnic minorities tripled from 20 million to 60 million. Between 1970 and 1990, they grew from one-eighth to one-fourth of the American population. This meant that by 1990 Blacks composed 12 percent of the population, Hispanics[2] 9 percent, Asians 3 percent, and indigenous peoples 1 percent.

Census Bureau projections indicate that the proportions of people of color will increase to almost half (48 percent) by the year 2050 (Bureau of the Census, 1992a). The Black and indigenous populations will double, the Hispanic population will triple, and the Asian American population will almost quadruple over the same time period. In contrast, the non-Hispanic White population will increase by only 5 percent.

The impact of these growing numbers of people of color is more evident at the local level (O'Hare, 1992). In seven of the ten largest cities in the United States, people of African, Latin American, Caribbean, and Asian backgrounds constituted more than one-half of the population in 1990 (see Table 1.1). Only Philadelphia, Phoenix and San Diego had a non-Hispanic White majority in 1990.

The increase of people of color at the local levels has been differential. Among the twenty largest cities, Blacks constituted the majority

TABLE 1.1

Race and Hispanic Origin in the 20 Largest U.S. Cities: 1990

City	Population (in 1,000s)	Percentage of Population				
		White	Black	Asian	American Indian	Hispanic
New York, NY	7,323	43	25	7		24
Los Angeles, CA	3,485	37	13	9		40
Chicago, IL	2,784	38	39	4		20
Houston, TX	1,631	41	27	4		28
Philadelphia, PA	1,586	52	39	3		6
San Diego, CA	1,111	59	9	11	1	21
Detroit, MI	1,028	21	75	1		3
Dallas, TX	1,007	48	29	2		21
Phoenix, AZ	983	72	5	2	2	20
San Antonio, TX	936	36	7	1		56
San Jose, CA	782	50	4	19	1	27
Baltimore, MD	736	39	59	1		1
Indianapolis, IN	731	75	23	1		1
San Francisco, CA	724	47	11	28		14
Jacksonville, FL	635	70	25	2		3
Columbia, OH	633	74	22	2		1
Milwaukee, WI	628	61	30	2	1	6
Memphis, TN	610	44	55	1		1
Washington, DC	607	27	65	2		5
Boston, MA	574	59	24	5		11

SOURCE: O'Hare (1992).

of the population in Detroit, Baltimore, Memphis and Washington, D.C. In San Antonio, Hispanics constituted the majority of the population at 56 percent contrasted with 7 percent for Blacks, 1 percent for Asian/Pacific Islanders and 36 percent for Whites. In San Francisco, there were more Asian/Pacific Islanders (28 percent) than Blacks (11 percent) or Hispanics (14 percent).

These growing population figures have been accompanied by a rise in political and economic power in the 1990s. At the national level, Latinos and Asian/Pacific Islanders have joined Blacks in reaching a critical mass necessary to create congressional caucuses. People of color are running for local, state, and national offices at unprecedented rates. Despite the disproportionate persistence of poverty for communities of color, an educated middle class with entry possibilities into corporate and suburban America has emerged for these groups.

THE INTERNATIONAL EXPERIENCE

Racial and ethnic group classification is not peculiar to the United States, for it exists in other societies. In April 1992, the U.S. Bureau of the Census and Statistics Canada convened an international conference on the measurement of ethnicity (Statistics Canada and the U.S. Bureau of the Census, 1993). Formal presentations were made by representatives from statistical agencies in Australia, Canada, Malaysia, Russia, the United Kingdom, and the United States. These agencies are faced with the task of how best to enumerate an increasingly heterogeneous population in a postindustrial, relatively mobile society.

A dominant theme of this conference was that ethnicity is constructed differently in each country. Construction was dependent on demography—how homogeneous or heterogeneous a country is, the state's ideas of inclusion or exclusion, and who decides what the officially recognized groups are. The distinguishing feature by which population groups are known is generally called ethnicity, but in fact this varies by country. For example, in Canada, the focus is on ancestry, reflecting the immigrant origins of most Canadians. In Malaysia, as well as in India and Indonesia, religion, language, and caste are definitive features. In the United States, attention is to skin color and blood quantum. Hispanic America and the Caribbean focus on language and culture. The official groups in the United Kingdom reflect the members of the British Commonwealth. Australia similarly reflects the British Commonwealth but also includes indigenous groups.

Some participants viewed race as a dimension of ethnicity while others mentioned ethnicity within the context of race. For non-Whites, race was viewed as holding equal or even greater meaning than ethnicity because race is the defining symbol of their unequal power relationship with Whites. Several participants stated that measurement of ethnicity is not a neutral task. It reflects a nation's need for selected data at various points in time. Hirschman (1993: 549) observed that "national systems of ethnic division and classification schemes seem more related to political history than to ancestry or cultural divisions."

Another type of ethnicity was recognized and named secondary ethnicity by Isajiw (1993) and other participants. Secondary ethnicity is attributed to groups whose geographic origins are distinct from their present birthplace and residence. That is, a group of people with common ancestry in one society migrates and exists for over several native generations in another society; examples are French Canadians, Black Britons, and Asian Americans.

Within the United States, the terms *nationality, race,* and *ethnicity* may be overlapping but are still distinct. Given a civic culture, nationality is based on citizenship. Race has been used to distinguish a White majority from a minority composed primarily of people of color. It has been imposed by the majority group. Ethnicity has been used mainly to describe White ethnics and is a form of self-definition not necessarily related to or based on a majority group. The ides of non-Whites as ethnic groups is not readily acknowledged (del Pinal, 1993).

THE RACIAL CLASSIFICATION
OF ASIAN AMERICANS

The formal classification of Asians in America as a racial category is relatively new. In governmental policies and statistical systems,

Asians in America were initially classified by subcategories of their national origin such as Chinese, Japanese, and Filipino. Prior to the 1990 census, data were available on a subgroup basis only. A total count of Asian Americans was not attempted until the 1980 census and this was based on sample data.

This subgroup classification is in direct contrast to the experience of the other groups, namely Whites, Blacks, and American Indians. These groups were initially identified as racial groups. It is only subsequently that their heterogeneity has become acknowledged. There is great variability among American Indian tribes. The Black population can be delineated in terms of American Blacks, Blacks from the Caribbean, and Blacks from Africa. The Hispanic population can be demarcated by various nationalities such as Mexican and Salvadoran.

The emphasis on Asian subgroups was not limited to the United States government but in fact was also encouraged by Asian Americans themselves. Realizing the great diversity of this population by nativity and national origins, Asian Americans have lobbied the Bureau of the Census and the National Center for Health Statistics to continue to collect data on specific nationality groups as well as a pan-ethnic category.

Another interesting feature of the racial classification of Asians in America is that it is rooted in geographical origins—the Asian continent. Blacks were not identified initially by their African origins but by their skin color. They were called colored folks or "Negro," the Spanish word for black. Similarly, American Indians were identified as red men and the more generic "indios," meaning native in Spanish, rather than by their tribal affiliations.

The formal classification of Asians in America as a racial group by the federal government coincided with the self-identification of Asian Americans as a pan-ethnic group in the 1970s and 1980s (Espiritu, 1992). In addition, just as Asian Americans have become more visible as a distinct political and demographic group, the issue of racial classification in the United States has become more complicated and called into question. The Asian American category encompasses a broad and varied range of populations from fourth-generation, upper-middle-class

Japanese Americans to newly arrived Southeast Asian refugees on welfare. Generalizations of such distinct populations must be made with caution. In addition, interethnic and interracial unions are increasing, especially among Asian Americans, calling into question the notion of mutually exclusive groups. Finally, the changing socioeconomic profile of Asian Americans is much closer to a non-Hispanic White majority than to other racial ethnic minorities.

While groups have been differentiated throughout American history, racial distinction has been subsumed under civil and economic status. A formal governmental policy to differentiate populations by racial category is relatively new. This policy, Office of Management and Budget Statistical Directive No. 15, Race and Ethnic Standards for Federal Statistics and Administrative Reporting, was promulgated in 1978.[3] While it has facilitated the reporting of data for minority racial and ethnic groups, including Asian Americans, its utility is being questioned. The debate over Directive 15 is whether this classification is outdated or irrelevant. This debate forces a closer examination of what defines an Asian American.

Because group identification does not occur in a vacuum but within the context of how a society defines groups, Asian Americans are examined in terms of the current racial and ethnic statistical policy. Chapters Two and Three are devoted to Directive 15. Chapter Two describes the origins of this classification, which includes Asian and Pacific Islanders. With Directive 15, the use of racial classification shifted from one of exclusion to one of explicit inclusion of specific groups. Chapter Three discusses the significance and continuing utility of this policy which has prompted Americans to look beyond the initial narrow racial classification of White and Black. Chapter Four focuses on Asians Americans as a racial category and minority group. Chapter Five addresses the multiplicity of identities of Asian Americans and draws the conclusion that Asian Americans may no longer be viewed solely as a racial category but as a pan-ethnic group which is defined beyond a majority/minority paradigm.

NOTES

1. The two-year residency requirement for naturalization was changed in 1795 to five years, in 1798 to fourteen years, and in 1802 back to five years.

2. Hispanics may be of any race.

3. The common date for this directive is 1977 when federal agencies were notified of this policy. The formal existence of this policy was its 1978 publication in the *Federal Register.*

CHAPTER TWO

DIRECTIVE 15 ORIGINS

Societal expectations do exist regarding fairness, equal opportunity, and specifically proportional representation, even
though we have not adequately dealt with questions of ethnic
and racial equality.

—David Fetterman (1988: 59)

As shown in Chapter One, racial and ethnic classification in the
United States was used initially to identify populations who were
excluded from full citizenship. By contrast, Directive 15 was developed
to ensure the inclusion of groups. Specifically, this directive defined
five basic standard racial and ethnic categories for federal statistical
and administrative reporting since 1978. Four were racial—American
Indian or Alaskan Native, Asian or Pacific Islander, Black, and White.
Two were ethnic—Hispanic and non-Hispanic. While the directive did
not preclude the collection of data for more detailed categories or
subgroups, it did require that such groups be reaggregated back to the
five basic categories.

DATA NEEDS FOR RACE AND ETHNICITY

The need for improved racial and ethnic data arose in three con-
texts. First was the persistent differential undercount of Blacks and

31

other racial minorities in the decennial census. For decades, the net underenumeration of non-Whites[1] has been and continues to be much greater than for Whites. In 1960, for example, among all males, 2.8 percent of White males were underenumerated compared to 10.9 percent of non-White males. Among all females, 1.6 of White females and 8.1 percent of non-White females were undercounted (Parsons, 1972: Table 1, p. 28). In 1970, the undercount rates were lower for both groups but the difference between the two groups stayed about the same with the rate of undercount for Whites at 1.9 percent and for non-Whites at 6.9 percent (National Research Council, 1978: Table 2, p. 2). There were two pressing reasons to diminish the differential undercount. The first was that an accurate and complete count of the total population is necessary for purposes of reapportionment of seats in the House of Representatives which is based on state population. Since the enactment of the Voting Rights Act in 1965, data are required on the racial and ethnic identification of people associated with specific geographic locations, namely residential addresses. The second reason to reduce the differential undercount was that decennial census data are the baseline for both federal and non federal statistics. The census is the benchmark of and denominator for most statistical systems.

The use of federal racial and ethnic categories, however, was not sufficient for reducing the undercount of racial and ethnic minority groups. In the 1990 Census, Blacks were undercounted by 4.8 percent, Hispanics by 5.2 percent, American Indians and Alaskan Natives by 5 percent, and Asians and Pacific Islanders by 3.1 percent.

A second context, difficult to ignore, was the growing self-consciousness and desire for recognition on the part of cultural, racial, and ethnic groups as American citizens and permanent residents. By 1950, the proportion of immigrants in the American population was 7 percent and in 1970 had decreased to less than 5 percent. In the post World War II era, second and third generations of Hispanics and Asians were increasing. Their identification was less with their countries of origin and greater with their country of birth. Along with Blacks and

American Indians, they stressed their inclusion in the American dream in a pluralistic society. These minority groups were beyond the assimilation perspective of the melting pot. Unlike Southern, Central, and Eastern Europeans, who by the third generation were considered White and American, racial minority groups remained distinct for several generations by their physical features and residential segregation. Throughout the 1950s and 1960s, racial minorities, with Black leadership in the civil rights movement, sought to end segregation in education, employment, housing, and public accommodations and services. The objective was integration of the races. The results, at best, were mixed, with resistance by some Whites to comply with new civil rights statutes. The integration of White schools in the South, exemplified by Little Rock High School in Arkansas, required the presence of federal officials from the Justice Department as well as federal troops to secure access for Black students. By the end of the 1960s, a younger generation of racial minority leaders, including Malcom X and Stokeley Carmichael, emerged to challenge the goal of integration. In the 1970s, the younger, U.S.-born generation called for Black Power and Brown Power. They sought self-identification and self-determination. An obvious manifestation of this self-consciousness was the rise of Black Studies departments on a variety of university campuses. At San Francisco State College, the School of Ethnic Studies, which encompassed Asian American Studies, Black Studies, La Raza Studies, and Native American Studies, was established in 1969.

As recently as 1970, the vast bulk of the U.S. population (98.7 percent) was composed of Blacks and Whites (U.S. Bureau of the Census, 1992b: Table 15). Asian Americans were less than 1 percent of the U.S. population.[2] Given this small proportion, what went unnoticed was that between 1960 and 1970 Asian Americans increased by 56 percent, from 878,000 to 1,369,00 (U.S. Department of Health, Education, and Welfare, 1974: 10). By contrast, the total U.S. population had increased by only 13 percent during this period. In areas of concentration such as San Francisco, Los Angeles, and Seattle, the Japanese,

Chinese, and Filipinos found themselves uniting as Asian Americans due to political and demographic changes (Espiritu, 1992: 25). The broader political context was the war in Southeast Asia and the civil rights movement, which heightened the racial consciousness of Asian Americans: "Americans of Asian ancestry united to denounce racist institutional structures, demand new or unattended rights, and assert their cultural and racial distinctiveness" (Espiritu, 1992: 25). Led primarily by college students, they formed the Asian American movement. College students were the children of immigrants united by their similar experience of growing up in the United States and sharing a common language, English. In areas of geographic concentration, they advocated for social services to their communities and relevant curriculum in higher education (Wei, 1993). The dilemma they faced in attempting to document social and educational needs was the lack of data specific to Asian Americans (US. Commission on Civil Rights, 1973: 5). For policy and planning purposes such data were limited. At most, data were available on White and Black and occasionally on Other or Oriental. In response to this dilemma, Asian American organizations and coalitions developed in the 1960s and 1970s pressing for local- and national-level data.

A major related but distinct context for racial and ethnic data was effective enforcement of federal civil rights legislation passed in the 1960s based on equal access and opportunity in public accommodations, governmental services, education, employment, and housing. According to the U.S. Commission on Civil Rights (1973: 3-4) in a review of the federal civil rights enforcement effort,

> racial and ethnic data are essential tools with which to combat discrimination and plan and monitor affirmative action to remedy past racial wrongs. . . . In addition to their significance in equal opportunity programs, general purpose racial and ethnic statistics are often indispensable as general background for policy formulation and program planning.

The commission noted that the Office of Management and Budget (OMB) acknowledged the utility of racial and ethnic data collection in federal assistance programs. The OMB recognized that to effectively carry out the policy of nondiscrimination, it was necessary for federal agencies to obtain considerable information on race (U.S. Commission on Civil Rights, 1973: 6). Despite this recognition, however, the OMB did not require that federal programs collect racial and ethnic data. Prior to the promulgation of Directive 15, limited direction relating to the racial or ethnic categories that should be used in federal statistics was provided by the OMB in Exhibit K to Circular A-46 "Race and Color Designations in Federal Statistics"[3] Although Circular A-46 provided some guidance for the collection of racial and ethnic data, it in no way ensured that data necessary for measuring distribution of program benefits to minorities would be collected.

Federal agencies provided minimal guidance to civil rights and program officials for tabulating, analyzing, or interpreting the data. Even those federal agencies requiring racial and ethnic data gave slight consideration to the question of who should use these data and how they should be used (U.S. Commission on Civil Rights, 1973: 8).

Among six federal agencies that the commission examined, only four—the Departments of Housing and Urban Development (HUD), Health, Education, and Welfare (HEW), Agriculture (USDA), and Labor (DOL)—held that procedures for collecting racial and ethnic data needed to be initiated for effective equal opportunity programs. The Department of Transportation (DOT) and the Veterans Administration (VA) did not have policies requiring agencywide collection of racial and ethnic data on beneficiaries of federal assistance programs.

IDENTIFYING RACIAL AND ETHNIC CATEGORIES

While the commission went into great detail about the need for racial and ethnic data, it also spent time explicitly identifying racial and ethnic categories and defining minority status. It noted that the USDA, HEW, HUD, DOL, DOT, and VA used six categories: White, Negro/Black, Spanish surnamed, American Indian, Oriental, and Other. These categories were based on a mixture of color, race, national origin, and ethnic designations. The commission went on to say,

> as commonly used, these designations do not refer strictly to race, color, national or ethnic origin, but rather to minority group membership perceived both by the particular groups and by the general public. As stated by HUD, racial, color and ethnic designations are now recognized and described as minority group.
>
> Separate classifications of race, color, national origin, or ethnic group can be justified only if the data which would result from such distinctions have a legitimate use in terms of combating discrimination, planning programs, or conducting program evaluation. . . . While statisticians have expressed the desire to separate color and/or race from ethnic or national origin group, minority groups do not express the need for such data. On the contrary, Spanish speaking groups, for example, express a great need for data on their members by country of origin such as Puerto Rican, Cuban or Mexican American. While persons of Spanish descent encompass all races, distinction based on national origin rather than race are seen as the meaningful ones.
>
> To some extent the problem relates to the choice of names for minority groups, and not to the decision of which groups should be separately identified. This problem arises as a result of the erroneous belief that minority group membership can be defined by the presence of particular characteristics such as skin color or language and that the names used to describe minority groups should reflect their individual characteristics. It is the essence of prejudice to expect that all members of a group bonded together by ancestry and common experience will share a single characteristic. The problem can be solved in part by selecting generally acceptable terminology which connotes minority group membership, but not necessarily minority group characteristics, and by providing clear definitions which indicate that the terminology is not intended to describe characteristics of all group members. (U.S. Commission on Civil Rights, 1973: 38)

The federal emphasis was clearly on minority status in a legal sense. Minority group status did not derive from a specific race or ethnicity per se but on the treatment of race and ethnicity to confer a privileged, disadvantaged, or equitable status and to gauge representation and underrepresentation. The example of age as a minority status may be helpful in understanding this distinction. Being a certain age does not necessarily in itself designate minority group status. When race is used as a criterion for excluding or restricting rights or opportunities, however, then minority status is conferred. Until recently, with respect to racial and ethnic groups, the overlap between minority status and selected racial and ethnic groups, namely American Indians, Asian Americans, Blacks, and Hispanics has been substantial, so that they appear synonymous when, in fact, any race or ethnicity, including Whites, may assume a minority status, such as in reverse discrimination cases.

Based on its findings, the U.S. Commission on Civil Rights (1973: 88) made several recommendations. One was that OMB should exercise strong leadership in the development and enforcement of a policy for the collection and use of racial and ethnic data, including establishment of governmentwide standards. The commission reasoned that through the budget examination process the OMB could ensure that federal agencies informed themselves of the extent to which their programs reached minority beneficiaries on an equitable basis.

Another recommendation was that federal agencies issue a policy statement supporting the collection of racial and ethnic data as necessary to combat discrimination against minority groups in the distribution of federal assistance. The commission further recommended a minimum set of categories—American Indian, Asian American, Black, Spanish Descent, and Other—to be used in programs of assistance and in general-purpose data collection. It went on to say that federal programs should be required to make provision for the collection of data on Cubans, Filipinos, Koreans, individual American Indian tribes, Portuguese, French Canadians, and other major concentrations of disadvantaged racial and ethnic groups when data collection takes place in the local communities in which significant numbers of these groups reside. The assumption by the commission was that these groups were, in specific situations, treated as minority group members and disproportionately underrepresented in access to resources.

HISTORICAL DEVELOPMENT
OF DIRECTIVE 15[4]

Prior to the issuance of the OMB Directive in 1978, variations of this policy were already being implemented by different federal agencies, including the former Office of Education and the Office of Civil Rights in the then Department of Health, Education and Welfare and the Census Bureau in planning for the 1980 Census. To develop standard racial and ethnic categories, the Federal Interagency Committee on Education (FICE) established the Ad Hoc Committee on Racial and Ethnic Definitions.[5]

In all these initiatives special attention was given to disparities between Black, Latino, American Indian, and Asian American populations in comparison to the White population based on existing Census data (U.S. Department of Health, Education, and Welfare, 1974; U.S. Commission on Civil Rights, 1978). These disparities were in large part due to earlier policies of limited or total exclusion in various areas such as citizenship, property rights, employment, education, housing, and immigration directed at these groups.

The promulgation of Directive 15 is based primarily on recommendations of the FICE and legislation such as P.L. 94-311, which Congress passed in 1976, requiring selected agencies to publish data on the status of Hispanics. In April 1975, the FICE released "The Report of the Ad Hoc Committee on Racial and Ethnic Definitions of the Federal Interagency Committee on Education." The report was a multiyear effort of federal agencies to develop "an integrated scheme of terms and definitions, conceptually sound which can be applied to cover major categories of race and ethnicity and can be used by all agencies to help meet their particular data requirements" (Federal Interagency Committee on Education, 1975: 20). The FICE proposed five categories: "American Indian or Alaskan Native, Asian or Pacific Islander, Black/Negro, Caucasian/White, and Hispanic." Additionally, it requested that the Bureau of the Census develop and conduct a field test to validate results and, if necessary, consider revisions to the categories and procedures for implementation. The final recommendation was that the OMB promulgate these categories and procedures as the standard for all federal agency data collection and reports on race and ethnicity.

Several controversial issues were considered by the Ad Hoc Committee, such as "Other Race, Mixed Race, race of Asian Indians, South American Indians, and observer-identification versus self-identification." Resolution of these issues was clearly interim, based on the relatively small proportions of these groups and their feasibility for inclusion in surveys at that time.

The Ad Hoc Committee considered the possibility of creating a category "Other," principally for individuals of mixed racial background and those who wanted the option of specifically stating a unique identification. Most committee members opposed the use of an "Other" category because it would complicate a survey and add to its costs:

> The Committee suggests that the number of legitimate responses to this category is likely to be small, particularly if the basic five categories are properly drawn and used. The use of an "Other" category requires the ability to edit "Other" responses carefully. Those which belong in the basic categories should be removed from this one. The number of responses in an "Other" category must be kept as small as possible or the usefulness of the survey would be adversely affected. (Federal Interagency Committee on Education, 1975: 17-18)

With respect to Asian Indians, the question at issue was whether to include them in the category Asian because they came from Asia and some were victims of discrimination in this country, or to include them in the White category because they were Caucasian, although frequently darker skinned than other Caucasians. The final decision favored the latter. The committee decided that while evidence of discrimination against Asian Indians existed, it appeared to be concentrated in specific geographical and occupational areas. Such persons could be identified in these areas through the use of a subcategory for their ethnic subgroups (Federal Interagency Committee on Education, 1975: 11-12).

With respect to the inclusion of South American Indians, some Ad Hoc Committee members felt that their definition should refer to the "original peoples of the Western Hemisphere" to provide for their inclusion. The committee eventually agreed, however, that the number of South American Indians in the United States was small and to include them might present data problems for agencies concerned with "Federal Indians" or those eligible for federal benefits.

On observer versus self-identification, the Ad Hoc Committee took the position that whenever possible, it was preferable for an individual to self-identify one's racial or ethnic background. There were instances, however, where this was not feasible, such as the HEW Office of Civil Rights school compliance survey. In such cases, an observer's determination of an individual's racial or ethnic heritage must be accepted (Federal Interagency Committee on Education, 1975: 13).

MAJOR COMPONENTS OF DIRECTIVE 15

In 1978, the OMB issued Statistical Directive 15, "Race and Ethnic Standards for Federal Statistics and Administrative Reporting." This policy provided standard categories for the collection and presentation of data on race and ethnicity in federal statistical and administrative reporting systems. Its intent was collection and use of "compatible, non-duplicated, exchangeable racial and ethnic data by Federal agencies."

The directive consisted of three components:

- Definitions for five basic racial and ethnic categories for federal statistics and program administrative reporting
- Designation of minimum data collection formats and types of reporting that would utilize these categories
- Instructions for data presentation

FIVE BASIC CATEGORIES

The directive defined five basic racial and ethnic categories for federal purposes: Americans Indian or Alaskan Native, Asian or Pacific Islander, Black, Hispanic, and White. The policy further stated that if separate race and ethnic categories were used the minimum race designation would be American Indian or Alaskan Native, Asian or Pacific Islander, Black, and White. The minimum ethnicity designation would be "Hispanic origin" or "Not of Hispanic origin."

For the most part, the OMB adopted the FICE Ad Hoc Committee report's recommendations. However, categories promulgated by the OMB differed in two ways from those of the FICE. First, while the five categories were retained, the terms Negro and Caucasian were dropped. Second, persons with origins from the Indian subcontinent were moved from the Caucasian/White category after the Association of Indians in America successfully lobbied to be included in the Asian or Pacific Islander category.

The racial and ethnic categories established by this policy were consistent not only with historical practice but also reflective of the American population of the 1970s. Whites were a numerical majority of the population and Blacks were the only sizable minority. This assumption was borne out in the 1970 Census data which indicated that Whites were 87 percent of the population and Blacks were 11 percent.

Together they comprised 98 percent. Asians were 1 percent. The remaining 1 percent was divided between American Indians, Alaskan Natives, and Other.

The choice of four racial categories and one ethnic category, however, redefined the U.S. population beyond a Black and White classification. This new classification facilitated the enumeration of a multiracial and multicultural population while preserving differential attention. The directive designated Whites as the majority group and Blacks as the principal minority group.

The particular status of the Hispanic population was recognized in two ways. Hispanic was the only choice for the ethnic category. Furthermore, in a combined racial/ethnic format, Black and White Hispanics were enumerated as Hispanics (but American Indians and Asian Hispanics were not recognized). The assumption here was that discrimination occurred due to Hispanic origin. In the case of Whites, this is intuitively appropriate, but in the case of Blacks it was questionable. Interestingly, what initially distinguished Hispanics from Spaniards was their mixed-race status based on Spanish descent and Indian ancestry.

In terms of definitions and identification, the directive was consistent with the FICE Ad Hoc Committee recommendations. Type of identification varied by category. All races were defined in terms of geographical region and ancestry, with additional methods provided for American Indians, Alaskan Natives, and Hispanics. American Indians and Alaskan Natives were identified by community recognition or tribal affiliation. Hispanics were identified by Spanish culture regardless of race. A minimal reporting format was to combine race and ethnicity so that there would be five categories—American Indian or Alaskan Native, Asian or Pacific Islander, Black, Hispanic, and White.

The directive was immediately effective for all new and revised record keeping or reporting requirements containing racial and/or ethnic information. All existing record keeping or reporting requirements were to be consistent with Directive 15 no later than January 1, 1980.

1978 SOCIAL INDICATORS REPORT

The relevance of these categories was reaffirmed in a study released by the Commission on Civil Rights in 1978. The groups examined were census categories consistent with those of Directive 15. The social indicators report was distinguished by its focus on the degree of inequality in the distribution of resources among various population groups. The emphasis was on minority and female interests. The social indicators of equality were oriented to the following concerns of women and minorities (U.S. Commission on Civil Rights, 1978: 3):

- Underdevelopment of human skills through delayed enrollment, nonenrollment in secondary education, and nonparticipation in higher education

- Lack of equivalent returns for educational achievement in terms of occupational opportunities and earnings

- Discrepancies in access to jobs, particularly those having greater than average stability, prestige, and monetary returns

- Inequality of income, relatively lower earnings for equal work, and diminished chances for salary wage increases

- A higher likelihood of being in poverty

- Proportionately higher expenditures for housing, less desirable housing conditions, restricted freedom of choice in selecting locations in which to live, and greater difficulty in attaining homeownership

Indicators were presented for different aspects of education, employment, income, and housing for men and women in the following groups: American Indians, Alaskan Natives, Blacks not of Hispanic origin, Mexican Americans, Japanese Americans, Chinese Americans, Filipino Americans, Puerto Ricans, and Whites not of Hispanic origin.

The indicators developed and presented in this report served two functions. First, they focused attention on some important and specific forms of equality. Second, they provided measurements of the degree of equality for these characteristics in 1960, 1970, and 1976, thus allowing a review of progress over this time period.

The general findings were broken into specific areas. The study found that in education, minorities and women were more likely to be behind in school, not enrolled in high school, without a high school or college education, educationally overqualified for the work they did, and earned less than comparably educated majority males.[6]

With respect to employment and occupation, women and minority males were more likely to be unemployed (especially teenagers), to have less prestigious occupations, and to be concentrated in different occupations than majority males. In terms of income, minorities and women had less per capita household income; lower earnings even after such determinants of earnings as education, weeks of work, age, and occupational prestige have been adjusted to equality among groups; smaller annual increases in earnings with age; and a greater likelihood of being in poverty.

Finally, minority- and female-headed households were more likely to live in central cities than the suburbs where majority-headed households live, less likely to be homeowners, more likely to live in overcrowded conditions, and more likely to spend more than a quarter of their family income on rent. Given these findings, the Directive 15 categories appeared appropriate. This was not the case, however, after ten years.

1988 PUBLIC COMMENTS

A decade later, in 1988, the OMB proposed a revision of Directive 15 as a part of governmentwide guidance for federal statistics to ensure that federal statistical activities were conducted as efficiently as possible.

"Guidelines for Federal Statistical Activities" was published in the *Federal Register,* Vol. 53, No. 12 (January 20, 1988). The purpose of these guidelines was to assist in ensuring that government-sponsored statistical activities produced statistics that were useful, accurate, and accessible to potential users and not unduly burdensome to respondents. The preamble to the draft circular did not discuss any specific reasons for the apparent changes to Directive No. 15, and it is difficult to determine whether substantive changes were intended or were the result of major editing.

As part of this effort toward simplification, the OMB recommended that the four racial categories be maintained but that a new category, Other, be included for persons who believed they did not fall into the preceding categories. It retained the ethnic categories of Hispanic and non-Hispanic. No rationale was offered for this change. No definitions were provided for any of the categories. The guidelines also reaffirmed that agencies could use more detailed categories as long as they could be reaggregated back to the basic categories.

As pointed out in public comments, the major changes in this revision were the lack of definitions for the categories and the redefinition of Other. In cases where an individual is of mixed racial and/or ethnic origins, Directive 15 already provided that the category "which most closely reflects the individual's recognition in his community should be used." A revision allowing Other would detract from the mutual exhaustiveness and exclusiveness of the basic categories.

Interracial organizations and individuals who questioned the exhaustiveness of the initial categories supported the inclusion of the Other category and specifically recommended that a mixed or multiracial category be included. They noted that there were between 600,000 and 5 million multi/biracial children in the United States (Multi-racial Americans of Southern California, 1988). This was clearly an increasing population.

However, federal agencies and nine congressional committees (Congress of the United States, 1988) registered disagreement with the proposed revisions. The congressional committees appreciated the fact that the designation of Other or Mixed Race would enhance feelings of self-identification and self-esteem by individuals, but they also pointed out that the current categories were necessary for the enforcement of civil rights laws. The committee chairmen noted that the proposed changes were particularly troubling from a civil rights perspective for two reasons: first, that the creation of a new category would result in a reduction in the current categories which were already underrepresented and undercounted, and second, that historical continuity of data would be disrupted and that measurement of the enforcement of civil rights law, over time, would not be possible.

Similar comments were voiced by federal agencies and external organizations. The federal agencies expressed concern that a new category would inadvertently cause confusion and inconsistent reporting. They were concerned that the collection and reporting of racial and ethnic data with an Other category would severely damage the accuracy and consistency of data used by several agencies in eliminating discrimination. They noted that this additional category would undermine the basic structure of the currently used categories and destroy the continuity of departmental statistical series. If specific provision was made to add the category Other, they recommended that it should be accompanied by a requirement to ask for specification as to what the individuals consider themselves to be (i.e., Other—specify _____) so that coding would permit many of them to be classified into the categories specified in Directive 15.

The Women's Legal Defense Fund (1988), the National Women's Law Center, and Women Employed asked a basic policy question: What treatment would the category Other be given for purpose of civil rights enforcement or compliance? Would Other or Mixed Race be counted as a protected category for the purpose of reporting affirmative action? The women's organizations noted that the racial and ethnic data collected pursuant to the OMB's directives were used not only by federal agencies but also by Congress and the private sector for a variety of reasons. The OMB had itself recognized that the collection of such data affects "people's lives and well being." The fund concluded that "any changes which may dilute the effectiveness of such efforts should be made only with extreme caution and for well developed and compelling reasons. Because the Office of Management and Budget has failed in its duty to provide such reasons, the proposed changes should *not* be implemented" (Women's Legal Defense Fund, 1988: 4).

Given the above responses, the OMB withdrew its proposed revision of racial and ethnic categories in 1988. Federal agencies continued to use the five racial/ethnic categories of Directive 15. Increasingly, state and local governmental agencies, marketing firms, private industry, and the nonprofit sectors also used this same classification.

The Directive 15 classification was compatible with prior and subsequent census classification. Prior to 1990, data collected were on subgroups. In 1960, specific groups were Chinese, Japanese, Filipino, Hawaiian, and Part Hawaiian (see Table 4.1 in Chapter Four). In 1970, Korean was added, and Part Hawaiian was deleted. Subsequent to Directive 15, several subgroups were added. In 1980, Vietnamese, Asian Indian, Hawaiian, Guamanian, and Samoan were included. In 1990, the category Other Asian or Pacific Islander was added. To comply with Directive 15, these subgroups could be aggregated into an Asian/Pacific Islander category.

Just as the Directive 15 classifications were becoming institutionalized with the 1990 census, documentation of a more diverse American society raised questions about the limitations of current racial and ethnic categories. By 1993, the federal government, particularly the OMB, was again revisiting Directive 15.

NOTES

1. In 1960, the color category "non-White" included Negroes, Indians, Japanese, Chinese, Filipinos, Aleuts, Eskimos, Hawaiians, part Hawaiians,

Asian Indians, Korean, Malayans, and other racial or ethnic groups of non-European or non-Eastern origin.

2. At this point, Asian Americans were predominantly Japanese, Chinese, and Filipino.

3. Circular A-46 sets forth procedures to be followed throughout federal departments and agencies to improve the gathering, compiling, analyzing, publishing, and disseminating of statistical information for any purpose. It was issued on March 28, 1952 by the Bureau of the Budget, the predecessor of the OMB. Exhibit K was issued on August 6, 1969.

4. This section is adapted from the prepared statement of Juanita Tamayo Lott at Hearings before the Subcommittee on Census, Statistics and Postal Personnel, April 14, 1993.

5. The OMB policy was based primarily on categories developed by the Federal Interagency Committee on Education and published in the "Report of the Ad Hoc Committee on Racial and Ethnic Definitions," April 1975.

6. Majority refers to Whites not of Hispanic origin.

CHAPTER THREE

CONTINUING UTILITY
OF DIRECTIVE 15

Government statistics commonly gain a momentum that expands their use into areas for which they may not be well suited.

—U.S. Commission on Civil Rights (1978: 3)

Among all racial and ethnic data collected and reported subsequent to the promulgation of Directive 15, the 1990 census produced more racial/ethnic/ancestry data that allowed individuals and groups to think of themselves beyond the policy-relevant context of Directive 15. This was due in part to the various combinations provided by the census but it was also due to the increased migration from countries in Asia, Africa, and Latin America most notably in the 1980s. In the context of self-definition, individuals could choose to identify or not identify with five racial/ethnic categories. This was the case for new immigrants, especially those from Africa, Asia, and Latin America, whose identities were based primarily on national origin (rather than race or Hispanic origin) and who lacked the discrimination legacy of their American counterparts. Individuals could also identify with more than one category. This was the case for the growing numbers of children of interracial and interethnic unions.

As the United States becomes more heterogeneous, the continuing utility of Directive 15 is again being questioned by federal statistical agency staff, academic researchers, human service providers, racial and ethnic communities, and even market researchers. Such questioning is healthy and timely. Such questions may even result in a new federal policy governing racial and ethnic categories. However, any proposed alternative should be made only with a clear understanding of the purpose and limitations of Directive 15. In addition, the significance of this policy should not be understated, even as its continuing utility is open to debate.

The directive represents the most current attempt to better classify racial and ethnic minority groups vis-à-vis a White majority group. It is not an absolute nor final standard and thus is subject to change. From a historical perspective, the current categories are relatively new and have been in use for less than two decades. The implementation of these categories has surfaced both the limitations and significance of this classification.

LIMITATIONS

The limitations of Directive 15 are on several levels. One entails the use of terminology for existing groups to reflect contemporary usage, such as "African American" for "Black." While these terms are not conceptually synonymous and point out the ambiguity and fluidity of labels, such changes do not threaten the existing classification. A second limitation is the inclusion of particular groups in a category. The most prominent example is the reclassification of Pacific Islanders from an Asian and Pacific Islander category to one that combines them with American Indians and Alaskan Natives. On the one hand, Pacific Islanders, particularly Hawaiians, share an indigenous status with American Indians and Alaskan Natives and specific legal relationships with the federal government. On the other hand, an Asian and Pacific Island category reflects a popular geographic usage of an Asian-Pacific region. These types of limitations are not insurmountable.

A more challenging limitation of Directive 15 is whether the current categories are exhaustive. Any new category undermines the current classification for it entails the addition of new groups who may neither identify with the current categories nor may identify as members of a minority group. Critics contend that a new category would diminish the numbers of existing groups. Nonetheless, the experience of the decennial census with the Other race category is not encouraging of new groups. While the numbers of the American population reporting in this category increased between 1970 and 1990 (from less than 1 million to almost 10 million) over 95 percent of persons reporting in the Other race category were Hispanic. In addition, despite the general perception of a sizable multiracial population about 253,000 (or only one-tenth of 1 percent of the population in the 1990 census) provided multiple race responses.[1] By contrast, in surveys that specifically include a multiracial category, the proportion rises to 1 to 1.5 percent (see OMB Findings section in this chapter).

Another limitation is whether the Hispanic origin category can continue to hold a preferential status. In distinguishing Hispanic origin as a separate ethnic category, Directive 15 set a precedence that selected ethnicity as primary over racial identity. Specifically, when a combination of race and ethnicity is used, Hispanics who are Black or White are excluded from the Black and White categories and counted under Hispanic. While Hispanics can be of any race, the White population in the past two decades has evolved to be defined as non-Hispanic.

Perhaps the most challenging limitation of this directive is whether such a policy has outlived its utility. In the current debate to revise Directive 15, the focus has shifted from measuring disparities between majority and minority groups to highlighting the benefits and entitlement of minority status. Such a shift may lead to the conclusion that disparities are minimal or no longer exist between the majority and minority groups, despite evidence that both continuation and reduction of disparities exist (see O'Hare, 1992; Harrison and Bennett, 1995). With emphasis on the latter, the monitoring of disparity and subsequent action to remedy disparities might no longer be primary policy objectives.

An equally popular reason for the outdatedness of this directive is that it does not reflect the groups with which individuals identify. New immigrants for example, identify primarily with their nationality rather than race or ethnicity. For other individuals, namely Whites, ethnicity is not primary to their identification and thus assumes an optional or voluntary status. Furthermore, in a heterogeneous society, persons can have a multiplicity of identities that are shaped not only by official categories but by the individual's self-identification and the definitions of a particular racial or ethnic community, by the media and the state. (Statistics Canada and the U.S. Bureau of the Census, 1993).

SIGNIFICANCE OF DIRECTIVE 15

Despite its limitations, Directive 15 has been a useful policy with administrative, conceptual, technical, and empirical significance. Federal agencies have found the directive useful for their data-collection and data-reporting activities. In turn, other governmental agencies at the state and local levels, as well as organizations in the private sector, have made extensive use of the directive for a variety of activities ranging from monitoring equal employment opportunity policies to the distribution of social services. The population groups identified by the Directive 15 racial and Hispanic-origin categories reflected legislative and agency needs and not efforts by population groups to be specifically identified.

Administrative Significance

Administratively, Directive 15 is significant in several ways. First, it evolved as the result of wide, multiyear, and thoughtful discussion among affected federal agencies. Second, it formalized and institutionalized independent and collaborative efforts of federal agencies to collect racial and ethnic data. It established five standard basic categories for the collection and representation of such data in federal statistical and administrative reporting systems. It also stated the types of federal reporting that would utilize these categories—civil rights compliance, general program administrative and grant reporting, and statistical reporting.

Third, because it emphasized basic categories and minimum standards, the directive provided a framework with latitude and flexibility for federal agencies to both expand or contract the basic categories based on their varied data needs. With respect to expansion, "in no case should the provision of this Directive be construed to limit the collection of data to the categories described above. However, any reporting required which uses more detail shall be organized in such a way that the additional categories can be aggregated into these basic racial/ethnic categories." In terms of contraction, the directive allowed for "collective description of minority races when the most summary distinction between the majority and minority race is appropriate." Interestingly, the term chosen for this group of minority categories was Other Races. Fourth, the categories were comparable with past census groups, allowing for some historical continuity and comparability.

Conceptual Significance

Conceptually, the significance of this directive was that it redefined race and ethnicity in ways to make them selectively inclusive and flexible to meet various federal policy and programmatic needs. This resulted in differential treatment of groups, as evident in the types of categories, the number of categories, and the kinds of identification allowed. This differentiation was a necessary factor in view of the range of inclusion and exclusion that various populations groups have been *subjected to* by the U.S. government and American society in general.

The choice of four racial categories and one ethnic category redefined the United States beyond a White and non-White classification and even beyond a White and Black classification. The new classification facilitated the enumeration of a multiracial and multicultural population. Differential treatment, however, continued to be given to Whites who were designated the majority group and to Blacks who were designated the principal minority group. The particular status of Hispanics was recognized in two ways. Hispanic was the only choice for the ethnic category. Furthermore, in a combined racial/ethnic format, Black and White Hispanics were enumerated as Hispanics. To avoid duplicated counts, the Black and White categories excluded Hispanics.[2]

In terms of definition and identification the directive was consistent with the FICE Ad Hoc Committee recommendations. Types of identification varied by category. While all the races were defined in relation to geographical region and ancestry, additional methods were provided for American Indians, Alaskan Natives, and Hispanics, among others. A final conceptual significance was the recognition of these categories as meaningful classifications despite the fact that they were neither mutually exclusive nor exhaustive.

Technical Significance

The technical significance of this policy was the ability and flexibility to collect, combine, and present a voluminous amount of data on many levels. Data could be tabulated by race and Hispanic origin separately or in combination. Each racial category could be further broken down by Hispanic origin. Specific subgroups within each of the race and Hispanic-origin categories could be enumerated and aggregated. Moreover, data on an Other category could be monitored. Rates of growth for each population could be tracked and estimated.[3]

The effective implementation of Directive 15, particularly in relation to noncensus data, however, has been mixed, suggesting that racial and ethnic data must still be used with great care and caution. In 1992, the General Accounting Office (GAO) reviewed the implementation of this policy in eight federal statistical agencies that collect significant amounts of racial and ethnic data and that receive such data from state and local sources. The GAO concluded that the agencies appeared to comply with the rules of Directive 15. However, it also found that agencies "do not verify compliance with the definitions by data collectors during the surveys because of the great demands on resources such an effort would require. This failure to verify compliance, combined with OMB's limited review, could be a source of error in reporting" (General Accounting Office, 1992: 3). For example, the National Education Longitudinal Study of 1988, a nationally representative sample of 25,000 eighth graders in more than 1,000 public and private schools, included West Asian (Iranian, Afghan, Turkish, etc.) and Middle Eastern (Iraqi, Israeli, and Lebanese) in the Asian or Pacific Islander category where they constituted 15 percent of this category. This is an incorrect designation under Directive 15, which includes persons from the Middle East in the White category.

Hahn's (1992) review of the federal system of health statistics— natality, morbidity, and mortality—found that terminology and procedures for collecting information differ within and among agencies that collect information, affecting the comparability and interpretation of resulting counts (Hahn, 1992) He cites as an example the inconsistency in coding race for births and deaths among U.S. infants who die before they are one year old. For White infants at birth, 1.2 percent were assigned a different race at death. By comparison, 4.33 percent of Black infants at birth and 43.2 percent of infants of other races at birth were assigned a different race at death.

Empirical Significance

The overriding significance of this policy is that it has resulted in a wealth of data not previously obtainable that captures the dramatic changes in racial and ethnic composition of the United States. Data

collected in accordance with this policy confirmed (1) the rising proportion of non-White groups, (2) the decreasing proportion of a White
majority, (3) the greater diversity across and within all groups, and (4)
the continuing, if changing, disparities between minority groups and
a White majority group. Such data further highlighted the expansive-
ness and limitations of current categories and the assumptions that
went into their development.

When Directive 15 was being formulated, racial and ethnic minorities were a stable but small proportion of the American population,
increasing from 10 to 20 million between 1900 and 1960. Between
1960 and 1990, however, with relaxation of immigration restrictions,
the numbers of racial/ethnic minorities tripled, from 20 million to 60
million. Between 1970 and 1990, they increased from about one-
eighth to one-fourth of the population. Census Bureau projections
indicate that this proportion will increase to almost half by 2050.

In the face of this voluminous data on race and ethnicity, two issues
have arisen. One is whether racial and ethnic data should be collected
at all, particularly at the national level and second, if so, whether the
current categories are still appropriate ones. According to Frank Weil
(1993: 3), who was a member of the FICE Ad Hoc Committee that
drafted Directive 15, much of the criticism leveled against racial cate-
gorization and the particular categories of Directive 15 has arisen because the categories are being used in areas never contemplated. He
cites as an example the radio and television talk show discussions of
partners in mixed-race marriages and their offspring and their difficul-
ties in determining to which category their children belong.

Directive 15 is the most current attempt to better classify racial
and ethnic minority groups vis-à-vis a White majority group in their
inclusion, representation, and distribution of a variety of resources
including, but not limited to, voting rights, public accommodations and
services, education, employment, and housing. It is neither an absolute
nor final standard for racial/ethnic classification per se. According to
proponents of Directive 15, it is the policy relevance of racial and

ethnic data that makes Directive 15 salient, not its possible use for identifying every population group that would like federal recognition. The dilemma is that the current categories may or may not be the ones with which individuals define themselves. From a strict civil rights perspective, the categories are appropriate for two reasons: first, because they do encompass race, color, and/or national origin, and second, because in discrimination cases, the relevant factor is how a victim of discrimination is perceived by the discriminator regardless of how an individual self-identifies. For example, persons of both White and minority race backgrounds may identify with both races. However, the historical tradition has been to view a person with minority group ancestry as non-White.

An opposite emerging view is posed by the multiracial movement. That is, that persons with minority group and White ancestry be defined as multiracial. Some states have enacted laws requiring the addition of new categories. Ohio and Illinois have passed legislation to add a multi-racial category on school forms that collect information on race and ethnicity. Georgia, Indiana, and Michigan have passed legislation requiring a multiracial category on all written forms and applications used by state agencies to collect information on race and ethnicity.

Despite the momentum for a multiracial category, the findings from a recent survey conducted by the National Center for Education Statistics indicate that the five standard federal categories are widely used by public schools:

> Approximately three-quarters of the nation's public schools specified that they use only the five standard federal categories to identify students' race and ethnicity. Fifteen percent of all schools reported using an "other" or "undesignated" category. . . . A general "multiracial" category is reportedly being used by 5 percent of all schools while 7 percent of schools are using additional racial and ethnic designations, such as "Filipino." Specific combinations of the five standard federal categories, such as "black/white" or an "unknown" category are

rarely used by schools to classify students' race and ethnicity (2 percent of schools). (U.S. Department of Education, National Center for Education Statistics, 1996: 6)

In almost three-fourths (73 percent) of all schools, parents or guardians had the opportunity to identify the race and ethnicity of their children. About a quarter of all schools assigned students to categories based on observation by a teacher or administrator. The majority of schools (84 percent) reported that less than 5 percent of their student population was inaccurately described by the five categories.

The debate on the continuing utility of measuring race and ethnicity occurs on both the national and community level. The first national forum was a set of hearings held by the Subcommittee on Census, Statistics and Postal Personnel in 1993. The second was a workshop on the federal standards for racial and ethnic classification held by the Committee on National Statistics at the request of the OMB. In addition, the OMB has held public hearings in various cities, including Boston, Denver, San Francisco, and Honolulu, and invited public comments on the review and possible revision of Directive 15.

HOUSE SUBCOMMITTEE HEARINGS

The House Subcommittee on Census, Statistics and Postal Personnel held a series of hearings between April 14, 1993 and November 1993 to consider not only modifications of existing racial categories but also the larger question of whether it is proper for the government to classify people according to arbitrary distinctions of skin color and ancestry. Chairman Tom Sawyer recognized the need for Directive 15 to serve federal purposes, but he also cited the need to address demographic reality. In opening comments he stated,

The racial and ethnic categories that the Federal Government measures serve a number of useful purposes. They include: compliance with the Civil Rights and Voting Rights Acts; tracking the huge demographic shifts going on currently; and tracking with health, education and economic data of all kinds.

We need to preserve the suitability of that data for all of those important applications. However, in an effort to preserve that kind of comparability, we have developed categories that, in the view of many, have become misleading over time.

They become categories of convenience that may not serve the purpose for which they were originally put in place. As a result, we craft an illusion of specificity, an illusion of precision where it may not exist.

In doing so, we may fail to capture what is really happening in a dynamic period in which patterns of change really are the singular characterization of an enormously diverse population. So there are harmful aspects to that kind of policy that we can address.

Finally, it is important to recognize that we are in a period of substantial demographic change. We don't want our standards of measurement to distort the intricacies of ethnic identity. We have to avoid over time the hardening of categories that don't inform us as well as they might, and become, as a result, increasingly irrelevant to many of the people we seek to enumerate. (Committee on Post Office and Civil Service, 1994: 1)

The focus of the hearings was on whether the five Directive 15 categories really continued to adequately serve their original purpose or whether a wider range of categories was needed to meet the requirement of the federal policies and laws that require enumeration. In essence, the hearings reviewed the executive branch's policy about which racial and ethnic groups should be officially recognized by the United States government. To ensure the broadest range of views, testimony was heard from various data users including federal agencies, researchers, traditional minority group organizations, and representatives of emerging or changing populations. The subcommittee also raised the questions whether the federal system was prepared to address issues like race and ethnicity categories that cut across the work of many different agencies.

While respondents welcomed the opportunity to revisit Directive 15, most viewed the existing categories as satisfactory minimal categories. Federal agencies did not recommend major revisions. In the case of the National Center for Health Statistics and the U.S. Commission on Civil Rights, the need was for additional detailed subgroups that could be collapsed back to the basic five categories. Arthur Fletcher, then chairperson of the U.S. Commission on Civil Rights, stated that in most cases of discrimination, additional detail on race and ethnicity was required for civil rights enforcement and policy determination. Manny Feinleib, then director of the National Center for Health Statistics, noted that the concept of race had many limitations for use in the health field. He pointed out that the four minority racial groups designated in Directive 15 differed in health status and their use of health services in highly complex ways that depended upon education, occupation, income, community environment, culture, and individual behaviors as well as discrimination and racism. In addition, for the purposes of disease prevention and health promotion, major considerations for identifying demographic subgroups also included commonality of language, homogeneity of health-related behaviors and attitudes, and group cohesiveness for mobilizing resources to address health problems and provide role models. Thus, it was often necessary to define racial and ethnic subgroups in much finer detail than specified by the current categories, even for the Black population (Committee on Post Office and Civil Service, 1993: 71).

Representatives from community-based organizations raised concerns about the ability to identify their own groups separately. They did not necessarily request replacement or elimination of current categories. These groups included multiracial persons, Hispanics, and Middle Easterners who did not identify clearly or consistently with any of the four major race categories. In addition, native Hawaiians requested inclusion in the Native American category, which encompassed American Indians and Alaskan Natives, and removal from their current inclusion in an Asian and Pacific Islander category.

In summary, participants expressed the need to work toward choices that reflect a modern, current understanding of how people identify themselves. Reception to the addition of new categories or regrouping within existing categories was coupled with a strong recommendation that any revision be subject to strict review and rigorous testing, particularly as to any unexpected effects on the current classification.

Sally Katzen, then administrator of the Office of Information and Regulatory Affairs in the OMB concluded that a comprehensive review of Directive 15 was warranted. She stressed comprehensiveness because these categories were not used simply for statistical purposes but for the federal government's many different needs for racial and ethnic data. She stated that it was essential to study the possible effects of any proposed changes to the categories on the quality and utility of the resulting data for a multiplicity of purposes:

> In summary, we recognize that it is time to review the current set of racial and ethnic categories. From the correspondence we have received, we have also come to understand with renewed poignancy that federal guidelines for classifying race and ethnicity represent for the public not simply an administrative or statistical procedure but more fundamentally a process that has deep personal significance for individuals. The challenge before us is to determine what revisions to the categories would be useful in the context of the federal government's many different needs for data on race and ethnicity, while at the same time promulgating categories and definitions that are readily understood and generally accepted by the public. (Committee on Post Office and Civil Service, Subcommittee on Census, Statistics and Postal Personnel, 1993: 220)

To initiate this comprehensive review, the OMB requested the Committee on National Statistics of the National Academy of Sciences to convene a workshop to stimulate informed discussion by a wide variety of data users on the current standards. It also established the Interagency Committee for the Review of the Racial and Ethnic Standards.

Finally, the OMB sought public comments on the standards for the classification of federal data on race and ethnicity in writing and public hearings.

WORKSHOP OF THE COMMITTEE ON NATIONAL STATISTICS (CNSTAT), NATIONAL ACADEMY OF SCIENCES

In February 1994, a national workshop was convened by the Committee on National Statistics. The purpose of the workshop was to stimulate informed discussion by a wide variety of data users on Directive 15. This broader focus was necessary since the federal standards were used beyond federal agencies. Data users included state and local governments, the research community, the private sector, and the non-profit sector. A major finding of the workshop was that the directive had become a strongly established standard for the collection and presentation of data on race and ethnicity for statistical, administrative, and compliance purposes. It was widely used and observed. Federal agency representatives noted that all federal agencies were affected by Directive 15. Most federal agencies reported favorably on the directive, although expressing a desire for specific guidelines. None suggested that it would be better off without a governmentwide standard (Edmonston, Goldstein, and Lott, 1996: 11).

Two major problems of the current standard were identified by workshop participants. One was that the current categories were not viewed by some participants as mutually exclusive or exhaustive. For example, persons from the Middle East did not necessarily identify with any of the categories, and multiracial persons did not want to choose only one category. The other major, recurring problem was the different counts of groups that resulted from different procedures. The standard allowed for two ways to identify race and Hispanic origin—as one question or two questions. In a one-question format, respondents could chooses from five categories: American Indian or Alaskan Native, Asian or Pacific Islander, Black not of Hispanic origin, White not of Hispanic origin, and Hispanic origin. In a two-question format, one on race and one on Hispanic origin, there was the opportunity to count Hispanics in the Black and White categories. Different counts also occurred between self-identification and observer identification.

Workshop participants articulated conflicting but important concerns. The first was that a federal agency classification needed to reflect the realities of a demographically changing American society yet serve its designated statistical and administrative purposes. Another was the concern of small populations to have separate counts while at the same time ensuring statistical reliability for smaller groups. A third was the need for continuity in categories for historical comparisons while adapting to changing demographics. A fourth concern was the need to monitor discrimination even as there was a need to de-emphasize racial and ethnic labeling. A final but underlying concern was the desire, particularly among the research community, for logical consistency in categories with the reality that the historical context defined such groups as American Indians, Blacks, and Whites by different criteria (Edmonston, Goldstein, and Lott, 1996: 3). Different populations were defined not just by race and ethnicity but by a combination of criteria. Initially, these criteria were in terms of free or slave status, color for Whites, and citizenship. Subsequently, they included color for Blacks, blood quantum for Blacks and American Indians, culture for Hispanics, community recognition for multiracial persons, nativity and generation for Southern, Central, and Eastern Europeans (immigrant parents and their offspring), and national origin for Asian Americans.

Given these concerns, the workshop agenda offered options for the collection and presentation of racial and ethnic data. There were four options regarding data collection:

- Eliminate the two-question format (one on race and one on Hispanic origin) in favor of one question with five racial/Hispanic categories

- Add new race and ethnicity categories for specific groups or for a multiracial identity

- Allow the collection of multiple responses, which would necessitate new procedures for reporting responses

- Use open-ended questions

Four options were also proposed for data presentation: maintain the current standard, make minor revisions to the existing categories, add new categories (that would not be collapsed into the current categories), or eliminate racial and ethnic classification altogether. The workshop participants concluded that whatever revisions were made to Directive 15 required research on racial and ethnic classification.

OFFICE OF MANAGEMENT
AND BUDGET FINDINGS

The issues raised by the congressional hearings and CNSTAT workshop were reiterated in oral testimony and written comments to the OMB between 1994 and 1996. The basic question that the OMB raised was whether the federal government should collect data on race and ethnicity. On the one hand, many federal agencies are required by federal statutes and regulations to collect racial and ethnic data. The legislative uses of decennial racial and Hispanic origin data alone number 60 citations (U.S. Bureau of the Census, 1991: 42-46). Many of the citations are specific to American Indian tribes and Alaskan Native villages. Others specifically mention minority and limited-English-speaking populations. Legislative uses of decennial data on ancestry number 14 and specify refugee and bilingual groups (U.S. Bureau of the Census, 1991: 46-47). It appears that racial and ethnic data may be collected for policy-relevant groups.

On the other hand, there are those who favor no collection of racial and ethnic data because doing so is divisive and unscientific and clearly not a function of the federal government. They contend that government should be concerned with citizenship data, not with race and ethnicity.

Another OMB finding was that

there are no clear, unambiguous, objective generally agreed-upon definitions of the terms, "race" and "ethnicity." Cognitive research shows that respondents are not always clear on the differences between race and ethnicity. There are differences in terminology, group boundaries, attributes and dimensions of race and ethnicity. Historically, ethnic communities have absorbed other groups through conquest, the expansion of national boundaries, and acculturation.

Groups differ in their preferred identification. Concepts also change over time. Research indicates some respondents are referring to the national or geographic origin of their ancestors, while others are referring to the culture, religion, racial or physical characteristics, language or related attributes with which they identify. The 1977 Directive No. 15 categories are a mix of these. These categories do not represent objective "truth" but rather are ambiguous social constructs and involve subjective and attitudinal issues. (Office of Management and Budget, 1995: 44680)

Based on a review of all criticisms and suggestions for changing Directive 15, the Research Working Group of the Interagency Committee established by the OMB identified issues for research and testing. Among the more significant were the classification of multiracial persons, combining race and Hispanic origin, combining concepts of race/ethnicity/ancestry; changing the names of current categories; and adding new classifications.

The Bureau of Labor Statistics was asked to design a supplement to the May 1995 Current Population Survey that would obtain data on (1) the effect of having a multiracial category among the list of races; (2) the effect of adding "Hispanic" to the list of racial categories; and (3) the preferences for alternative names for racial and ethnic categories. There were mixed findings from this study. In terms of the inclusion of a multiracial category this addition resulted in a decrease in the proportion of American Indians, Eskimos, or Aleuts from .94 percent to .73 percent when there were separate race and Hispanic-origin questions and from 1.06 percent to .79 percent in a combined race and Hispanic question (U.S. Department of Labor, 1995: Table 2). With respect to Hispanic origin, a higher percentage of persons identified themselves as Hispanics when they were asked a separate Hispanic question than when "Hispanic" was included as one category in the race question. While the proportion for Blacks and Asians or Pacific Islanders was not significantly affected by the introduction of either the Hispanic or the multiracial options in the list of racial categories, there were a couple of surprising findings. The proportion of Blacks increased from 10.29 percent to 10.66 percent with the inclusion of a multiracial category. Yet the proportion of Asian or Pacific Islanders decreased from 3.83 percent to 3.25 percent with the inclusion of a multiracial category (U.S. Department of Labor, 1995: Table 2). With respect to terminology, the majority of Hispanic respondents chose Hispanic as the preferred term. A large plurality of Blacks preferred the term Black but almost as many chose African American or Afro-American. While the majority of American Indian or Alaskan Native respondents preferred the term American Indian or Alaskan Native, over a third chose Native American. Almost three of ten multiracial respondents preferred the term Multiracial, but about as many had no preference. About 1.5 percent of the population responded Multiracial when this category was included (U.S. Department of Labor, 1995).

The National Content Survey, conducted between March and June 1996 by the Bureau of the Census, also tested alternative versions of the questions on race and Hispanic origin. Three treatments were involved: the addition of a multiracial response category in the race questions, placement of the Hispanic-origin question immediately before the race question, and the combination of both these changes (U.S. Bureau of the Census, 1996). Regarding the multiracial category, about 1 percent of respondents reported that they were multiracial when this response category was included. Over 80 percent of the multiple write-ins in the multiracial category included White. A high proportion—30 percent—were Asian or Pacific Islander responses. About 25 percent involved a Black response and about 7 percent an American Indian response. The bureau made the following observation:

> Given that only one percent of persons reported as multiracial, the effects on larger race groups are small. For example, even if all those who reported as multiracial and who included White among their write-ins had instead reported a single race of White, the percentage increase in the White proportion of the population would have been only one percent. The comparable increase for Blacks would have been three percent. In contrast, if the Asian and Pacific Islander write-ins to the multiracial category had been reported solely as Asian and Pacific [i]slander, the proportion of the population in that category would have increased by more than 10 percent. (U.S. Bureau of the Census, 1996: 25)

While this study found that the addition of a multiracial category had no statistically significant effect on the percentages of other races, it noted that there were declines in the proportions reporting as Asian and Pacific Islander when a multiracial category was included. In the two panels where the race question preceded the Hispanic-origin question, 4 percent of respondents were Asian or Pacific Islander when there was no multiracial category. When a multiracial category was included in the second panel, the proportion of Asian or Pacific Islander decreased to 2.7 percent (U.S. Bureau of the Census, 1996: 26).

The 1996 Race and Ethnic Targeted Test, which is the principle test of questions on race and ethnicity, also found that the addition of a multiracial category to the race question and the provision of instructions to "mark all that apply" reduced reporting of Asians and Pacific Islanders in the targeted sample (U.S. Bureau of the Census, 1997: 25).

In summary, the results from the Current Population Survey supplement, the National Content Test, and the Race and Ethnic Targeted

Test suggest that the provision of multiracial options may well affect reporting in populations with high intermarriage rates, most notably Asians and Pacific Islanders. Although these findings are preliminary, they do suggest two trends: a variety of responses to racial and ethnic identification and fluidity in how persons respond. Emphasis today is on self-identification and being recognized as a distinct group, regardless of historical or current minority status.

In deciding whether there will be any changes to Directive 15 and subsequently to racial and ethnic questions for the 2000 Census, the OMB is now considering research findings and public comments on race and ethnicity. A decision from the OMB is scheduled before 1998 when the dress rehearsal for the 2000 Census occurs. In sum, while the continuing utility of present categories is questioned, development and maintenance of a revised set of categories is not an easy task.

NOTES

1. This is limited to write-in responses to the Other category and includes responses such as "biracial" and "multiracial." The Census Bureau recoded specific responses of more than one race to the first race. For example, responses of Black/White were recoded Black. Responses of White/Black were recoded White.

2. This procedure ignores the possibility of Hispanic American Indians and Hispanic Asians and Pacific Islanders.

3. The collection and presentation of this voluminous and unprecedented information is due in large measure to the pioneering technical efforts of the Census Bureau in consultation with affected groups and federal agencies.

CHAPTER FOUR

ASIAN AMERICANS: A RACIAL CATEGORY

The classification of Asians in America as a racial category is a relatively new concept, with the term "Asian American" coined only thirty years ago. It has been used ambivalently, even reluctantly by some Asian and Pacific Americans because it describes a large and very heterogeneous population. At the same time, the term is now used with growing familiarity among non-Asian and Pacific Americans. The promulgation of Directive 15 accelerated that familiarity. With a national racial category, local efforts to define an Asian American population were validated and made official.

MINORITY GROUP STATUS

Although the racial category Asian American is relatively new, the status of Asian Americans as a minority group can be traced back to 1790. Like Blacks and American Indians, Asian Americans were differentiated from Whites by their legal status. The racial minority group status of Asian Americans stems from their historical definition as "aliens ineligible for citizenship." The first naturalization law in the United States, the Naturalization Act of 1790 passed by the first U.S. Congress, set up criteria for citizenship which were explicitly racial. The two main qualifications were that the alien have resided for two years in the United States and be a free White person.

According to Lesser (1985-1986: 84-85),

> The racial component of the first law went unchallenged until after
> the Civil War. In 1870 Congress passed a new naturalization act
> which added the new racial category of "aliens of African nativity and
> persons of African descent" to those eligible for naturalization. . . .
> Thus, in effect, the act was a Republican compromise which explicitly
> excluded Chinese, so that persons of African descent might become
> citizens. It was a compromise which joined together Easterners, who
> had no "Chinese problem" and Westerners whose main concern was
> the Chinese. The compromise had important consequences. After
> 1870 with freed Blacks eligible for naturalization, Asian immigrants
> became the more significant "other" in terms of citizenship eligibility.

On the basis of race and national origin, the Chinese and other
Asians were denied U.S. citizenship. This status was maintained in state
and federal laws for almost a century. The Naturalization Act of 1790
became the basis for many laws directed against Asian Americans ow-
ing land or business, attending schools with White students, and living
in White residences. As Shinagawa noted (1996: 85), "By using the
language of 'aliens ineligible for citizenship,' local, state and federal
governments could discriminate specifically against Asian Pacific
Americans without naming them directly, which would otherwise subject them to prosecution under the 14th amendment." Only in 1952
with the passage of the McCarran-Walter Immigration Act were Asians
allowed to become naturalized citizens.

The minority group status of Asian Americans was furthered reinforced by immigration laws restricting their entry as U.S. residents.
In 1882, Congress passed the Chinese Exclusion Act which suspended
immigration of Chinese laborers. Those who were not lawfully entitled
to reside in the United States were subject to deportation. This act was
followed by the 1907 Gentleman's Agreement which restricted immigration of the Japanese. In 1917, immigration restriction was extended
to other Asians with the creation of an Asian-Pacific Triangle or barred
zone that extended from China and India to the Pacific Islands of

Polynesia. With the 1924 National Origins Act, Asian immigration was virtually nonexistent. The act established quotas at 2 percent of the total members of each nationality residing in the United States according to the 1890 Census.

Foreigners

The minority group status of Asian Americans was further reinforced by popular images of them as foreigners and enemies. On one hand, Blacks and Whites are considered the primary settlers of the United States, American Indians and Alaskan Natives indigenous to this land, and Hispanics, as descendants of Spanish America, indigenous to the Southwest and the Caribbean. On the other hand, the prevailing image of Asian Americans is that they are alien to this country.

This image was found even among the first Chinese, Japanese, and Filipino immigrants who saw themselves as sojourners or temporary contract laborers, not unlike some Eastern, Central, and Southern Europeans. Their initial intent was to earn money in the United States and return to their Asian homelands. Only the early Japanese immigrants were able to become permanent settlers. They were able to immigrate not just as single males, which was the general case for the Chinese and Filipinos, but as family units. Japanese women came as picture brides in the early twentieth century to labor alongside their husbands in the fields of Hawaii and California.

The historical sojourner has several modern counterparts. One are Asian nationals, such as Japanese nationals, who live, work or study in the United States for several years. They have no intent to reside permanently in the United States but do, however, view their American experience as integral to their careers. Another type of sojourner are adult immigrants and refugees who have arrived in the United States since 1965. The majority of these persons are expatriates. While their intent is to be permanent U.S. residents and citizens, they are equally or primarily interested in the politics and situation in their homelands.

For them, home is Asia, not the United States. Upon retirement, some expatriates return to their countries of origin.

The image of foreigner can also be found among highly skilled and better-educated immigrants who are part of the Asian diaspora. They view themselves as quite cosmopolitan and beyond national boundaries. Born in Asian lands, mainly former colonies, they may have been educated in France, Great Britain, the United States, or other former colonial powers. Subsequently, such individuals may work in another country, oftentimes in international or multinational organizations, and perhaps claim residence in yet a third county. Examples are Asian British, Asian Canadian, Asian African, and Asian Caribbean. These individuals migrate to the United States and find that they are viewed as Asian American, although they may not necessarily identify as such.

Although Asian Americans have obtained naturalization rights, their continuing image as an alien or foreigner reinforces their minority group status. Increasing immigration during the 1970s and 1980s resulted in the growth of the foreign-born population. As late as 1970, the majority of Asian Americans were born in the United States. By 1980, however, over half (59 percent) were born in other countries. By 1990, two-thirds of the Asian American population was foreign born. By comparison, the total foreign-born population numbered 20 million, or 8 percent of the U.S. population. The new immigration came primarily from Asia, Mexico, and other parts of Latin America, with Asians and Latinos constituting two-thirds of the foreign-born population. Almost 38 percent of Asian Americans entered the United States between 1980 and 1990.

Enemies

At selected times in history, such as during wars and times of economic depression, Asian Americans have been viewed as the enemy. During the Great Depression in the 1930s, racial and ethnic minorities were viewed not only as competition for jobs but also as competition for social services. Filipinos who were at the time nationals in the United States and technically not aliens were deported to the Philippines. Mexican Americans, born in the United States, were similarly repatriated to Mexico. In the 1990s, with the downsizing of jobs in the corporate and public sectors and cutbacks in social service budgets, immigrants, of whom Asians and Hispanics comprise a substantial portion, once again have become the targets of anti-immigration policies (Hing and Lee, 1996).

Many of the wars fought by the United States in the past 100 years have been in Asian lands—the Spanish American War in the Philippines; World War II fought partly in Japan, China, and the Philippines, the Korean War in Korea, and the Vietnam War in Vietnam, Cambodia, and Laos. The most vivid example of racialization of Asian Americans is the World War II evacuation and internment of West Coast residents of Japanese ancestry based on Executive Order 9066. Signed by President Roosevelt in 1942, the order authorized the Secretary of War and designated military commanders to prescribe military areas from which any or all persons may be excluded. The order did not specify that it applied only to persons of Japanese descent. Its effect, however, was on the Japanese American community. Of the 110,000 Japanese American internees, two-thirds were American citizens by birth and the rest were permanent residents. They were treated as prisoners of war, even though no charges were brought against them and claims of a threat to national security were unsubstantiated. No comparable action was taken against German or Italian Americans despite the fact that Germany and Italy were also at war with the United States.

Hate Crimes

In the 1980s and 1990s, Asian Americans were once again viewed as labor competition and a drain on resources. Dramatic increases of immigrants and refugees in the Asian and Pacific Islander population occurred just as the American economy declined. Between 1980 and 1990, this population doubled while U.S. manufacturing industries experienced major layoffs and corporations were downsizing. During this period there was an increase in the occurrences of anti-Asian activity that included vandalism, harassment, intimidation and violence. According to an audit by the National Asian Pacific American Legal Consortium (1995: 1), there was over a 35 percent increase in reported anti-Asian incidents between 1993 and 1994—from 335 in 1993 to 452 in 1994. The current level of anti-Asian sentiments is also anti-immigrant. A significant number of hate crimes included references to going back to the country of origin.

Racial antagonism is directed at both immigrant and American-born Asian and Pacific Americans. In New Jersey, hate groups such as the Dotbusters and Edison Boys have organized against Southeast Asians. Vietnamese and Cambodian refugees in Massachusetts and Chicago are fearful, as are Korean store owners in New York City and Los Angeles. Over 3,000 Asian-owned businesses were targeted by rioters in the 1992 Los Angeles riots, which erupted after the Rodney King trial. Internationally, U.S. trade competition with Japan has resulted in "Japan bashing." Asian and Pacific Americans are identified with Japanese nationals. This blurring of different ethnic and nationality groups due to anti-Asian sentiment reinforces the racial category of Asian Americans.

AMBIGUITY OF MINORITY GROUP STATUS

While the historical treatment of Asian Americans as a minority group is clear due to explicit and implicit statutes and policies of exclusion, their recent and continuing minority group status is one of ambiguity. While the minority group status of Blacks, Hispanics, and American Indians is a given, the minority group status of Asian Americans is sometimes questioned. This ambiguity is in part due to the type of relations that the United States has with Asian countries and to the socioeconomic status of Asian Americans.

During World War II, when Japan was a major foe of the United States, Japanese Americans were denied their civil rights. Japanese American citizens on the West Coast were treated as aliens.[1] At the same time ironically, the United States government fostered the inclusion of other Asians as American permanent residents and citizens. China was an ally of the United States, and the Philippines was an American territory. Chinese and Filipino American soldiers were granted naturalization rights in 1943. Immigration was encouraged with the repeal of exclusionary laws and the enactment of such acts as the 1946 War Bride Act, which allowed entry of Asian wives of American servicemen under a nonquota category (Mark and Chin, 1982: 99).

The minority status of Asian Americans has also been questioned due to their general socioeconomic status. The higher educational attainment and median family income of Asian Americans, relative not only to minority groups but also to a non-Hispanic White majority group, are cited as indicators of success and therefore sufficient reason to view Asian Americans as a nonminority. For example, in 1990, over 78 percent of all Asians 25 years old and over were at least high school graduates. This compares to a national rate of 75 percent. The college attainment of Asians is more impressive and almost double that of the American population. Almost 38 percent of Asians had a bachelor's degree or higher compared with 20 percent of the general population (U.S. Bureau of the Census, 1993a: Table 3). What is less known, however, is that this high educational attainment in large part reflects Asians who have immigrated to the United States as professionals and family members of professionals. A significant number of Asian immigrants enter the United States with higher-level skills and graduate degrees earned in their homelands.

With respect to income in 1990, the median income of Asian and Pacific American households was $36,784 compared with $30,056 for all households (U.S. Bureau of the Census, 1993a: Table 3). The income of Asian and Pacific American families in 1990 was higher on average than that of White families. The median family income of Asian and Pacific Americans married-couple families was $42,259 compared to $36,920 for White families (Bennett, 1992). Per capita income, however, was lower for Asian and Pacific Americans— $13,638 compared to $14,143 nationwide (U.S. Bureau of the Census, 1993a: Table 3). These income figures must be viewed with the reality that the Asian and Pacific American population is concentrated in some of the most expensive metropolitan areas such as Honolulu, San Francisco, and New York. Their relatively higher income is due partly to the higher cost of living where they reside. Also, on average, Asian and Pacific Americans have larger size families and more workers per household working more hours to earn their income. They also have higher rates of poverty compared to non-Hispanic Whites.

Perhaps the most visible challenge to the minority status of Asian Americans is higher education, specifically the admissions of Asian Americans to elite universities, such as the University of California at Berkeley, Stanford, Princeton, and Harvard. As noted by Takagi (1992) controversy over this issue began in the 1980s. The Asian American population had more than doubled in size between 1970 and 1980. This growth was reflected in higher education as application and enrollment rates of Asian Americans rose. At the University of California at Berkeley, undergraduate enrollment of Asian Americans quadrupled between 1966 and 1980—from 5 percent in 1966 to 20 percent by 1980 (Takagi, 1992: 21).

Despite this increase, Asian Americans made two claims of undergraduate discrimination. One was that their enrollment rates were lower rather than proportional to their application rates. The other was that their admission rates were lower than that of Whites (Takagi, 1992: 23). On both coasts, Asian Americans questioned whether there was a quota imposed on them in higher education.

The Early Meanings of an Asian American Concept

The Asian American concept exists not as an absolute phenomenon but in relation to other settlers and residents of the United States. It is defined internally by members and externally by outsiders. Self-definition is at both the individual and group level. Observer-definition historically has been provided by a White majority society. As the United States becomes more heterogeneous and the proportion of racial/ethnic minorities increases, it is conceivable that observer definitions will also be made by other minority groups.

The early meaning of "Asian American" was made by Asian Americans themselves to define persons of Asian ancestry who were American permanent residents and citizens and to distinguish them from a White majority while acknowledging commonality with other racial and ethnic groups. Contrary to popular belief, the term Asian American was not decreed by governmental or other external authorities. It was coined mainly by U.S.-born Chinese, Filipino, and Japanese college students and community-based human service organizations on the West Coast and in New York (Wong, 1972; Wei, 1993). Many of these students and human service workers were second- and third-generation Americans. They viewed their ethnic communities as primarily composed of working-class immigrant grandparents, immigrant and American-born parents, and American-born children. They considered themselves Americans, not expatriates of Asian countries nor second-class citizens. With immigration from Asia virtually closed in the first half of the twentieth century, cultural ties with Asia were not actively reinforced. At that time, newly arriving immigrants were still a minority. U.S.-born Asian Americans experienced American culture in everyday life, even if only in marginal ways. The lesson from the World War II internment of Japanese Americans was to stress an American, not an Asian, identity—namely, to emphasize citizenship, not alien status.

Survival by means of accommodation to mainstream society was a logical strategy for a very small and vulnerable population. Growth of Asian American communities was limited to natural increase. However,

given their few numbers and disproportionate ratio of males to females, growth was minuscule. Speculation arose about the lack of the
formation of Filipino American communities and the disappearance
of Chinese American communities. By 1949, sociologist Rose Hum
Lee (1949) could write about the decline of Chinatowns. As recently
as 1960, there were less than 1 million Asian Americans in a nationwide
population of 180 million.

While the first meaning of "Asian American" emphasized "American," it also encompassed the relative status of Asians in America. It
was a concept that came into existence as a response to being distinct
from other Americans. Historically, Asian Americans viewed their
communities as a minority relative to a White majority. By the 1960s,
however, they also viewed themselves in relation to other racial/ethnic
minority communities and to Asians in Asia. Many had grown up in
segregated neighborhoods with Blacks, Latinos, and American Indians.
Their identification with Asians was sharpened with the 1965 Immigration Act and the prolonged war in Southeast Asia which, taken
together, increased the numbers of immigrants and refugees from Asia.
By 1969, formal recognition of the term Asian American was given in
the establishment of Asian American Studies programs in institutions
of higher education, namely San Francisco State College, the University of California at Berkeley, and the University of California at Los
Angeles,

In the 1970s, Asian American was joined by the term Asian and
Pacific Americans. This expanded concept was developed as Asian and
Pacific American communities, residing primarily in contiguous neighborhoods on the West Coast, formed coalitions to advocate for representation in federal, state, county, and municipal programs. A variety
of professional organizations formed Asian/Pacific caucuses, many of
which are still active. A few national Pan Asian organizations emerged
such as the Pacific/Asian Coalition and the Organization of Pan Asian
American women. Relative to the diversity of Asian and Pacific Americans
today, Asian and Pacific Americans in the early 1970s seemed to be a

clearly defined group. Heterogeneity described a finite number of ethnic groups. Emphasis was on being American—that is, born and reared in the United States and U.S. citizens and permanent residents.

A second meaning of Asian American was made popular by researchers and the media which defined Asian Americans separately from other racial/ethnic minorities in the 1970s. This was the meaning of a model minority. Rather than highlighting their similarities with racial and ethnic minorities, the meaning of Asian Americans as a model minority stressed compatibility with White majority values and standards of success. This included a strong work ethic and a high value placed on education. This meaning treated Asian Americans as a homogeneous population, when in fact the basis for this definition was not all Asian Americans but selected groups of high achievers, such as second- and third-generation Japanese Americans and Chinese Americans. The model minority was used as an example for other racial minorities, mainly Blacks and Hispanics, to aspire to. Thus, Asian Americans were defined as separate from a White majority and from other racial and ethnic minorities. Moreover, the model minority meaning persists for selected new immigrants, such as high-achieving Asian Indians, Vietnamese, and Taiwanese, even as it continues to be challenged as a myth by Asian Americans.

In summary, the early meaning of "Asian American" was made by Asian Americans to (1) define persons of Asian ancestry who were American permanent residents and citizens and (2) distinguish them from a White majority while acknowledging commonality with other racial and ethnic groups. A second early meaning was provided by the dominant society to distinguish Asian Americans from both a White majority and other minority groups.

Current Meaning in Federal Policy

These early meanings can be found to some extent in current federal policy. The relative status of different groups, including Asian

Americans, is maintained specifically in OMB Statistical Directive 15. All groups are defined in terms of geographical region, ancestry, and/or minority or majority status. Whites are persons with origins in any of the original peoples of Europe, North Africa, or the Middle East. Blacks are persons having origins in any of the black racial groups of Africa. Asian and Pacific Islanders are persons having origins in any of the original peoples of the Far East, Southeast Asia, the Indian subcontinent, or the Pacific Islands. American Indians, Alaskan Natives, and Hispanics have additional unique definitions. American Indians and Alaskan Natives are persons having origins in any of the original peoples of North American and who maintain cultural identification through tribal affiliation or community recognition. Hispanics, defined indirectly by geography (Spain), are persons of Mexican, Puerto Rican, Cuban, Central or South American, or other Spanish culture or origin regardless of race.

The nongeographic definitions provided specifically for American Indians, Alaskan Natives, and Hispanics suggest selective and relative status among these groups. The selective definitions for other racial/ethnic groups in the United States reinforced the secondary status of Asians in America relative not only to a White majority but to other racial/ethnic minorities. It should be noted that the federal statistical policy does not directly recognize Asian Americans per se. Rather, it defines Asian and Pacific Islanders as persons of Asian and Pacific origins. Although Directive 15 did not address nativity, it reinforced the immigrant alien status of Asian Americans because of its focus on geographic origins.

Directive 15 bolstered extant but uncoordinated efforts toward inclusion and equal representation on behalf of Asian Americans. Many of these efforts began in the early 1970s in the U.S. Department of Health, Education and Welfare (DHEW, now the Department of Health and Human Services). At the policy level, the Division of Asian American Affairs in the Office of the Secretary was responsible for cross-cutting programs, research, and employment issues (1971-1981). The Asian and Pacific Concerns Staff of the Office of Education (1976-

1982) focused on educational programs and policies. In the 1970s, the Social and Rehabilitation Services and the National Institute of Mental Health appropriated several million dollars to a variety of research and demonstration projects at the local and national levels.[2] Subsequent to an analysis of the 1970 Census data by the DHEW, the Bureau of the Census created the Asian and Pacific American Advisory Committee for the 1980 Census. The broad representation of the committee members was manifested in the choice and number of Pan Asian groups itemized in the 1980 Census form.

The Department of Justice, the Equal Employment Opportunity Commission, and the Office of Civil Rights in the Department of Education (formerly the Office of Education) utilize the Asian and Pacific American category for compliance and enforcement activities. The Commission on Civil Rights (1979) conducted a national consultation and issued state advisory committee reports on this population. The Small Business Administration, lobbied by community groups and legislators, included Asian and Pacific Americans as an eligible category for programs for disadvantaged small businesses. By these actions minority group status was no longer defined primarily as a civil status but was made synonymous with the racial category Asian American.

Demographic Data on Asian Americans

Demographic data on Asian Americans did not exist per se until the 1990 Census. Since 1870, national data on Asian Americans were by subgroup. As shown in Table 4.1, these subgroups varied from census to census. It was only in 1990 that a complete count of Asian and Pacific Islanders was obtainable from the census short form asked of all households. In 1990, the census race question included for the first time an Asian or Pacific Islander banner under which were listed Chinese, Filipino, Hawaiian, Korean, Vietnamese, Japanese, Asian Indian, Samoan, Guamanian, and a write-in category for Other Asian or Pacific Islander.

			Other Asian or	
Year	Chinese	Japanese	Pacific Islander	Other
1870	Chinese			
1880	Chinese			
1890	Chinese	Japanese		
1900	Chinese	Japanese		
1910	Chinese	Japanese		Other + write in
1920	Chinese	Japanese	Filipino, Hindu, Korean	Other + write in
1930	Chinese	Japanese	Filipino, Hindu, Korean	Other race, spell out in full
1940	Chinese	Japanese	Filipino, Hindu, Korean	Other race, spell out in full
1950	Chinese	Japanese	Filipino	Other race, spell out
1960	Chinese	Japanese	Filipino, Hawaiian, part Hawaiian, etc.	
1970	Chinese	Japanese	Filipino, Hawaiian, Korean	Other (print race)
1980	Chinese	Japanese	Filipino, Hawaiian, Korean, Vietnamese, Asian Indian, Samoan, Guamanian	Other (specify)
1990	Chinese	Japanese	Filipino, Hawaiian, Korean, Vietnamese, Asian Indian, Samoan, Guamanian, Other Asian or Pacific Islander	Other race

TABLE 4.1

Asian/Pacific Islander Categories in the U.S. Census: 1870 to 1990

SOURCE: Edmonston and Schultze (1995: Table 7.1).

As recently as the 1970 Census, data were available only for four Asian groups—Chinese, Filipinos, Koreans and Japanese—and one

Pacific group—Hawaiians. Together they totaled about 1.5 million or less than 1 percent of the U.S. population. The Japanese and Chinese constituted the majority of the Asian American population (38 percent and 28 percent, respectively). In the 1970 Census, the majority of Asian Americans were born in the United States. Ninety percent resided in urban areas. Well over half lived in California or Hawaii.

By contrast, based on sample form responses, the 1980 Census identified twelve Asian American groups (Asian Indian, Cambodian, Chinese, Filipino, Hmong, Indonesian, Japanese, Korean, Laotian, Pakistani, Thai and, Vietnamese) and five Pacific Island groups (Guamanian, Hawaiian, Melanesian, Samoan and Tongan). Due to the increase of Asian immigrants and refugees throughout the decade, the Asian American population more than doubled from 1.5 to 3.7 million persons. They were still less than two percent of the U.S. population. Ninety-five percent of the Asian American population was distributed among six groups—Chinese (23.4 percent), Filipinos (22.6 percent), Japanese (20.7 percent), Asian Indian (11.2 percent), Korean (10.3 percent), and Vietnamese (7.1 percent). By the 1980 Census, the majority (59 percent) of Asian Americans were foreign born.

In 1990, Asian and Pacific Americans numbered 7.3 million, representing 2.9 percent of the U.S. population. About 66 percent were born in foreign countries, and the same percentage lived in five states—California, Hawaii, New York, Illinois, and New Jersey. Their regional concentration continued, with about 60% living in only three states—California, Hawaii, and New York. This concentration is noteworthy in view of dispersal policies in recent decades. The most notable are the evacuation of Japanese Americans from the West Coast to other regions during World War II and the post-1975 resettlement of Southeast Asian refugees throughout the United States. Today, however, Asian Americans are a highly urban/suburban group. In 1990, only 6 percent of Asian Americans lived outside metropolitan areas compared to 25 percent of non-Hispanic Whites. The Census Bureau estimates that in 1996 there were 10 million Asian and Pacific Americans, or

3.7 percent of the American population. In 2000, Asian and Pacific Americans are projected to be 11 million, or 4.1 percent of the total population.

Changing Meanings With Current Data

Of all federal statistical systems, the Census Bureau has provided the most flexibility for collection of subgroup data. It has also employed a mutual process for defining racial and ethnic groups through such vehicles as advisory committees for the decennial census composed of members for each of the four minority racial/ethnic groups. For the Asian American population, census data has meant not just enumeration but detailed characteristics for an ever increasing number of subgroups. This increase is not due only to improved data collection procedures but to the tremendous immigration from Asian counties in the past twenty years. Relatives of earlier settlers—primarily working- and middle-class Chinese, Filipinos, and Koreans—come to be reunited with their families. Moreover, immigration policies directed to competitive labor force needs and humanitarian policies had also permitted the entry of new Asian Americans—notably poverty-level Southeast Asian refugees—and highly educated and highly marketable professionals and entrepreneurs, such as the Taiwanese and Asian Indians. Such diversity in a short time period has expanded the coverage of "Asian American."

Census Bureau work on the ancestry item suggests an even greater number of subgroups. This work defines Asian ancestry differently from Directive 15. Over forty groups composed of Asian countries, regional groups (e.g., Cantonese, Okinawans) and interracial groups (e.g., Eurasian, Amerasian) were identified in the 1990 Census. These groups were then aggregated by geographical origin. The federal policy on racial and ethnic categories limited Asian origins from an area bounded by the Pacific Ocean up to and including the Indian subcontinent and defined persons of Middle East origins as White. The

Census Bureau classification of Asian ancestry, however, is arranged by three geographic categories—South Asia, Other Asia and North Africa and Southwest Asia (U.S. Bureau of the Census, 1992c: Table D). The first two categories include the more traditional groups captured in the race item, but the third category includes persons of the Middle East. Similarly, Census Bureau work on foreign-born data includes Middle East countries as Asian. This classification is consistent with immigration and naturalization data but inconsistent with Directive 15.

What is occurring is that the early meanings of Asian American are being superseded by a new focus on two groups: new immigrants and multiracial persons. Such persons compose a growing proportion of the Asian American population. New immigrants from Asian lands and cultures may or may not view themselves as members of a racial minority category or a pan-ethnic category because they do not share the legacy of historical discrimination nor group solidarity with American-born Asians. Multiracial persons are questioning the need to be defined as a member of only one group. In addition they are not limited to a category that connotes minority group status. Their call for recognition is not as a historical racial minority group but as an emerging group distinct from historically defined racial and ethnic groups.

The focus on subgroups by Asian Americans (rather than the federal government) began during the planning for the 1980 Census when the Asian and Pacific Islander Census Advisory Committee strongly recommended a listing of various nationality groups under the Asian and Pacific Islander category. Composed of community members representing programmatic, policy and research backgrounds, the committee argued successfully that new immigrants would not necessarily relate to a generic Asian category. The recommendation was reiterated by the 1990 Census Advisory Committee and adopted, despite bureau field tests on the reliability of a generic Asian and Pacific Islander category (General Accounting Office, 1993). This suggests that the Asian American community itself is actively redefining and reassessing group identification. At the same time, a reordering of geographical categories in terms of ancestry and foreign-born items by federal statistical systems demonstrates a continuing redefinition by outside parties, notably national institutions.

NOTES

1. Interestingly, Japanese Americans in Hawaii were not interned because they constituted a substantial proportion of the population and labor force. The Hawaiian economy was dependent on the labor of Japanese Americans.

2. These include the Pacific/Asian Coalition and the Asian America Mental Health Research Center.

CHAPTER FIVE

ASIAN AMERICANS: A MULTIPLICITY OF IDENTITIES

Asian Americans in the United States were first defined not as a racial category or ethnic group but as a legal status. For almost a century they were defined as aliens ineligible for citizenship. During World War II, Japanese Americans in particular were defined, for all intent and purposes, as prisoners of war. German Americans and Italian Americans with a similar status—that is, ancestry in a country with which the United States was at war—did not. With the passage of sweeping civil rights legislation and court cases in the 1950s and 1960s, there was a shift in the identification of Asian Americans as well as other minority populations. The minority populations became synonymous with racial categories. The protected categories were no longer just a civil status but specific racial and ethnic groups which were formalized in Directive 15 and operationalized in federal programs and policies.

In the 1990s, another shift has occurred that questions whether populations can continue to be classified only, or even primarily, by racial and ethnic categories. This shift is from group identity based on racial category to individual identity based on a given situation. An implicit assumption for using racial and ethnic categories is that race and ethnicity are primary to one's identity. In fact, individuals have a multiplicity of identities of which ethnicity or race may or may not be primary.

INTERNATIONAL AND
HISTORICAL PERSPECTIVES

Decisions as to which population groups are officially recognized historically have been made by governmental agencies, politicians, and statisticians. In recent years, several industrialized countries, including the United States, Canada, and the United Kingdom, have held consultations with affected racial/ethnic groups and a broader range of data users (Statistics Canada and the U.S. Bureau of the Census, 1992). Such discussions have yielded several observations on the nature of race and ethnicity.

One is that the distinguishing feature by which population groups are known is generally called ethnicity. In fact, this varies by country as mentioned in chapter one. Group identity is based on various characteristics which have included ancestry, national origins, color, religion, language, culture, and caste. In the United States, attention has been on skin color, blood quantum, and shared historical experience of exclusion.

A second observation is that ethnicity has different meanings for different groups. It varies by whether the meaning of ethnicity is optional or definitive. For example, for Whites in the 1990s, ethnicity may be voluntary and symbolic. That is, ethnicity is not necessarily a primary or salient identity for some White Americans (Lieberson and Waters, 1988). In a postindustrial society, such as the United States, ascriptive features such as sex, race, and ethnicity may not be as germane to one's group identity as in primarily agricultural and industrial societies Rather, achieved characteristics such as educational attainment and profession may form the basis of primary group identity.

For non-Whites, however, ethnicity and race are defining characteristics with a level of intensity that varies according to level of discrimination and perception of extinction. Furthermore, Whites are viewed as ethnic groups and allowed to have ethnic pride, whereas non-Whites are considered ethnic categories structured around race, tribe, and nativity. This focus is viewed not as ethnic pride but as racial or ethnic politics (del Pinal, 1993; Petersen, 1983). In the United States, pan-ethnic groups in this view are not only, or even primarily, products of shared cultural bonds but of political and social processes (Espiritu, 1992) that define groups relative to a White majority. The formation of pan-ethnic groups is initially a response to a shared, exclusionary treatment as a minority group by the majority rather than common bonds of heritage. It is only subsequently that there is an evolution of a pan-Asian culture expressed through the arts and literature and embodied in institutions such as Asian American Studies.

A third observation is that race and ethnicity may be relative rather than absolute, and ethnic status may be achieved rather than ascribed. Race and ethnicity may be fluid over the life cycle of an individual as well as for the group. A related observation is that the racial or ethnic group to which an individual belongs is not limited to a state's officially recognized groups or to media images. Race and ethnicity are also dependent on the self-definition of an individual and the acceptance of that individual by the group. How people think of themselves and how they are treated by the state, the media, and the group itself affect whether individuals choose to identify with a group. Whether an individual is recognized as a group member is evident in the case of American Indian tribes where membership is based on specific and varying tribal definitions.

Finally, whether a country is inclusive or exclusive of selected groups relates to its apparent preference to maintain a homogeneous society or to operate as a multicultural or multiracial society. A review of census forms indicated that several countries' official, original view focused on homogeneity (or a melting pot perspective), but over time, and particularly in the past decade, heterogeneity (cultural diversity) has become a growing reality. Although the original intent for identifying selected groups may have been for purposes of exclusion or restriction, the present trend is toward inclusion for at least three reasons: to accurately reflect a diverse society; to implement policies that promote multiculturalism, and to measure disadvantage and discrimination. For example, due to national policies such as the Multiculturalism Act of 1988 and equal employment legislation of 1986, Statistics Canada is mandated to provide data on multiculturalism and employment equity programs by various racial ethnic groups (White, Badets, and Renaud, 1993). Equal opportunity policies were developed in the United States based on civil rights statutes on public services, employment, education, and housing in the 1960s. They were followed by workforce diversity policies in the 1990s, with the view that differences by race and ethnicity are potential strengths for promoting work productivity. In a multicultural and multiracial society, racial and ethnic differences are not barriers but assets and reasons for celebrating diversity.

NATIONAL PERSPECTIVE

The experience in the United States is both toward assimilation and greater diversity by race and ethnicity. There is some evidence that Whites find their European ancestry to be decreasing in significance. This is a process to be expected as massive assimilation occurs to the point of no longer knowing (or at least reporting) one's European origins. About 12 percent of respondents in the 1980 Census and about 10 percent in the 1990 Census gave "American" as their ancestry. In their analysis of the 1980 Census data on race, ethnicity, and ancestry, Lieberson and Waters (1988: 250) found that

> as ethnic identity declines as a sociopolitical issue for White groups and as it loses the influence it once had on major life chances and behaviors, two processes seem to result. First, a proportion of the population also changes their identification—identifying as "American" or "unhyphenated White." Second, although the majority of the populations still report at least one European ancestry, many of these reports appear to involve distortions of the full array of their ancestral roots. For many respondents, the ethnic origin(s) they choose to re-

port is becoming a choice made from within the set of ancestries in their histories.

This suggests that race and ethnicity among majority group members may become optional identities over time and by situation. Asian Americans may be in a transitional state as they are ambiguously considered both a minority and a majority.

By contrast, the influx of new immigrants since 1965, particularly from non-European countries, has brought about a resurgence of pride in national origins and the reporting of detailed ancestries. For these groups, such as Central Americans and Arab Americans, current racial and ethnic categories are insufficient to describe the American population. The official racial/ethnic categories reduce the U.S. population to five groups at a time when traditional and new populations express a need to go beyond these categories. Asian Americans have been the most effective group in lobbying for and obtaining a racial category and specific ethnic groups in the decennial census.

ASIAN AND PACIFIC AMERICAN
LEVELS OF GROUP IDENTITY

Just as "Asian American" is gaining common usage as a pan-ethnic category relative to other groups, Asian and Pacific Americans are emphasizing their heterogeneity. This diversity is not only by ethnic groups but by a multiplicity of identities. While a pan-ethnic or racial category is acknowledged by Asian Americans, such a category is not viewed as a replacement or substitute for specific ethnic groups. For now, identity as a racial category continues to persist, even after several generations. It coincides, however, with several other identities.

In a study of Asian and Pacific Americans in the Washington, D.C. area, several levels of group identity were identified (Lott, 1989). The most basic identity was the self-contained or village mentality found among the newest arrivals from rural and low socioeconomic back-grounds. At this level of identification, one's immediate family, clan or tribe is the primary frame of reference. This identity was found among Southeast Asian refugees. At this level, there may be little or no con-nection with an ethnic or national identity in their country of origin. Not surprisingly, they do not readily identify with an Asian and Pacific American category when they immigrate to the United States. A second level of identity is primarily regional but also linguistic or religious affili-ation. Sometimes, these subgroupings take precedence over the ethnic group identity, as in the case of Filipinos who identify themselves as Tagalog, Ilocano, or Visayan before identifying themselves as Filipino.

The next level of identity was in terms of an ethnic group, ancestry, or country of origin. It was an identity shared across socioeconomic groups, despite length of residence in the United States. Immigrant and U.S. born respondents spoke of the need to preserve an ethnic identity and not blend into an Asian and Pacific American identity, let alone a purely American one. This was not a rejection of a pan-Asian identity but a realization that the latter was an additional, not a surrogate, identity. The distinction of this identity is that it is not dependent on the definition of other groups. In contrast, the racial category Asian American is defined in relation to a White majority and other racial minorities.

A bicultural identity was found within two groups. The first is the "1.5" generation coined by Rumbaut and Ima (1988) in their study of Southeast Asian refugee youth. It described children born in Southeast Asia but raised and educated, for the most part, in the United States. It also describes other foreign-born Asian Americans, such as young Korean Americans who are most similar to U.S.-born Asian Americans. That is, their primary identification is being an American with Asian heritage. A second bicultural group can be viewed as a "half and half" generation, which describes persons who grew up in Asia but came to and resided in the United States for a good portion of their adulthood, including graduate school. They are familiar with both Asian and American identities and cultures. The communities from which they come include others like them but also persons who identify more as Asians and others who identify more as Americans.

Another emerging identity is an interethnic or pan-Asian one, which is the result of interethnic unions within the Asian American population. Whereas in previous decades interracial union were more common, mostly as a White/Asian phenomenon, interethnic marriages are becoming visible in areas where large numbers of Asian Americans reside (Shinagawa and Pang, 1996). An interethnic identity is relatively new and challenges attempts of Asian Americans to maintain discrete subgroups while simultaneously uniting under an Asian American category. Asian Americans are no longer only various national origins subgroups lumped together in a larger racial category. They are marrying across the Asian subgroups and are forming new groupings such as Japanese/Korean and Filipino/Vietnamese. A common combination is Chinese/Japanese. These individuals are truly pan-Asian.

Beyond the pan-Asian identity is a growing but very small class of persons with a global identity transcending ethnicity or race because of multilingual skills, residence in more than one country, and a higher rate of interethnic and interracial marriages. What this suggests is a view of Asian and Pacific American populations unbounded by national borders as, for example, the "overseas Chinese" and "Asians in the Americas."

The identity of Asian Americans is complex and encompasses all the above levels of identities. A person may choose to identify one way over another in a given situation. As Espiritu (1992: 15) notes, "a person is a Japanese American or an Asian American, depending on the ethnic identities available to him or her in a particular situation." For example, when one is the only Asian American in a group, the appropriate identity is as a racial category. Among a gathering of different Asian Americans, an ethnic group response would be more likely.

This multiplicity of identities is not limited to Asian and Pacific Americans but has variations in other racial and ethnic groups. American Indians, for example, are defined not just as a racial category but by tribes. Among the Black population, there is growing identification with geographical background including the Caribbean, Africa, and the United States.

THE CONTINUING VIABILITY OF AN ASIAN AMERICAN CATEGORY

Given the emerging multiplicity of identities, can an Asian American category continue to be viable? It must be noted that the viability of an Asian American category has been questioned since its inception. The definition of "Asian American" has been fluid, erring on the side of inclusiveness, on the assumption that persons of Asian and Pacific ancestry share a common history of discrimination and exclusion in the United States. This commonality, however, was challenged in the 1970s by Filipinos in California who lobbied successfully for a "Filipino" category distinct from an "Asian American" category. The rationale, in part supported by 1970 Census state data, was that Filipinos held a lower socioeconomic status than other Asian Americans, namely the Chinese and Japanese.[1] A distinction was made between "yellow" and "brown" Asian Americans. It could be argued that the status of Filipinos was more akin to Pacific Islanders in the sense that the Philippines and Pacific Islands had been U.S. colonies. This raised the question whether Filipinos were Asian Americans or Pacific Islanders or a separate category. While this issue was debated at local levels,[2] Filipinos continued to be included in an Asian American category at the national level. About this same time the Asian American category was expanded to become the Asian and Pacific Islander category.

The Case of Asian and Pacific Americans

The birth of the Pacific/Asian Coalition in 1972, the first pan-Asian national organization to receive a major federal grant from the National Institute of Mental Health, paved the way for an Asian and Pacific Islander category. Asian American organizations were transformed into Asian and Pacific American organizations in competing for federal funds. In lobbying for racial categories for the 1980 Census, Asian and Pacific Islander community representatives joined forces on the Census Advisory Committee for Asian and Pacific Islander populations. While the committee strongly recommended individual group categories, it did not object to the umbrella category. Data presentation for the 1980 Census was in terms of "Asian and Pacific Islander."

In contrast, by the 1990 Census the differences between Asian and Pacific Islander communities were more visible than their commonalities. Pacific Islanders requested a separate data presentation. First, they constituted a small and decreasing proportion of the Asian and Pacific Islander population. In 1980, there were 260,000 Pacific Islanders, compared to 3.5 million Asians, or about 7 percent of the total Asian and Pacific Islander population. In 1990, there were 365,000 Pacific Islanders, compared to 6.9 million Asians (U.S. Bureau of the Census, 1993c: Table 3), a decrease to 5 percent. While the Pacific Islander population grew 41 percent between 1980 and 1990, the Asian population grew by 99 percent. Second, the demographic profile of Pacific Islanders was quite different from Asians. In 1990, most Pacific Islanders, of whom more than half were Hawaiian, were primarily native born. Only 13 percent of Pacific Islanders were foreign born. In contrast, 66 percent of Asians were born in foreign countries. The family size of Pacific Islanders of 4.08 persons was higher than the 3.79 persons per family for Asians.

With respect to age, the Pacific Islander population was younger, with a median age of 25 years. Asians had a median age of 30. Pacific

Islanders also differed from Asians by educational attainment and income. The combined educational attainment of Asians and Pacific Islanders is relatively high, with 41.9 percent of males and 31.8 percent of women holding at least a bachelor's degree. These figures mask the lower educational attainment of Pacific Islanders, for whom in 1990 only 12 percent of males and 9.6 percent of females held at least a bachelor's degree. With respect to income, the per capita income of Asians in 1990 was $13,806 and for Pacific Islanders $10,342.[3]

In preparation for the 2000 Census, the Asian and Pacific Islander category is again evolving. Among native Hawaiians, there is a movement to be enumerated not in a separate Pacific Islander category but with American Indians and Alaskan Natives on the basis that native Hawaiians are indigenous to the Americas. This proposal has been submitted for consideration by native Hawaiian organizations to the Bureau of the Census and the OMB (Office of Management and Budget, 1994). For the most part, Asian American organizations are supportive of, or at least not in opposition to, such a movement. Yet some American Indian groups oppose the addition of a native Hawaiian category, noting the legal relationship between the United States government and American Indian tribes (Edmonston, Goldstein, and Lott, 1996: 31).

It is ironic that an Asian and Pacific Islander category is being questioned in the 1990s just as organizations such as the Asian Pacific American Legal Consortium, the Congressional Asian Pacific American Caucus Institute, and the Asian Pacific American Labor Alliance are recognized as national Asian and Pacific American organizations with a presence in Washington, D.C.

At this point, the shift of Pacific Islanders to another racial category does not challenge the viability of the Asian American category. Two categories, however, do: Multiracial and Transnational. Both of these categories could preempt the Asian American category. The Multiracial category is in distinct opposition to a classification of discrete categories. The Transnational category would supersede an American context of racial minorities.

Multiracial or Interracial Identity

Asian Americans face the reality that they are creating a new race—and a new world. Historically, colonial legacy and the continuing presence of American military and businessmen in Asia and the Pacific region have brought forth many Amerasian children. Closer to home, the second, third and fourth generations of Asian Americans are participating in mainstream activities, including marriage and families. A notable number of Asian American men and women in visible and leadership positions are married to spouses of other Asian and Pacific American groups and outside the Asian American population.

The emerging meaning of persons of mixed origins is to classify them as distinct from either parent and from any of the major racial and Hispanic-origin categories. This is a departure from Directive 15 and the historical and current procedures of the Bureau of the Census and the National Center for Health Statistics which provide for only one category. Directive 15 instructed that persons of mixed racial and/or ethnic origins should be classified by the category in which an individual is recognized in his community. Both the Bureau of the Census and National Center for Health Statistics historically categorized persons of biracial or multiracial backgrounds as the racial minority.[4]

The most obvious example of mixed populations are the Amerasian children, a designation to describe the children of U.S. servicemen and Asian women. These children have existed since the first American military intervention in Asia in 1898 during the Filipino revolutionary war against Spain. They were made visible by the children of veterans of the Vietnam War and formalized in the Amerasian Homecoming Act of 1987. Another emerging example are mestizos: Asians who are Hispanic. While existing federal policy requires collecting data on Black and White Hispanics, there is no policy acknowledging Asian Hispanics. Nevertheless, the 1990 Census indicated that over 4 percent of Asian and Pacific Islanders were of Hispanic origin. By contrast, less than 3 percent of Blacks were of Hispanic origin.[5]

Finally, in 1980 among all Asian and Pacific Islander children under 18 years of age living with both parents, over 10.6 percent were interracial. This is a higher rate than for comparable White children at 1.2 percent and Black children at 2.4 percent. Only American Indians and Alaskan Natives at 35.8 percent had a higher proportion of interracial children (Bennett and Robinson, 1993).

The multiracial issue is of concern to Asian Americans and other racial minorities. In recent years, the movement to include a multiracial category in the federal racial and ethnic classification has resurfaced. Much of the impetus has been at the local and state levels (see Chapter Three). Multiracial organizations have lobbied the OMB to include a multiracial category in the federal racial and ethnic classification system. While this issue has gained prominence, the data on a multiracial population suggest that it is a small but growing population. In 1990, one-tenth of 1 percent, or 250,000, were enumerated as multiracial, based on write-in responses to an "Other" race category. In 1995, in a May Current Population Survey supplement, which included a separate multiracial category, between 1.65 and 1.55 percent of persons enumerated were multiracial (U.S. Department of Labor, 1995: Table 2). In a survey of public schools, about 5 percent of schools used a general multiracial category. It also found that "in general, most respondents reported that various suggested revisions to the five standard federal categories were not an issue or were only a minor issue in terms of their applicability to students enrolled in their schools." (U.S. Department of Education, 1996: iv). Proponents of the multiracial category state that although they do not identify with the current categories, they do not question their continuation but do request an expansion of categories and/or the ability to check more than one category. Opponents though view the multiracial category as a challenge to the existing federal categories of Directive 15, arguing that persons previously categorized under Directive 15 would move to a new multiracial category, thereby depleting numbers from the current federal categories.

The dilemma of the multiracial category was summed up by Henry Der (1994: 96) on behalf of the National Coalition for an Accurate Count of Asians and Pacific Islanders:

> Like individuals of single race groups, persons of biracial or multiracial backgrounds seek acknowledgment and identification through the race question. Because existing federal civil rights laws and programs are premised largely on exclusive membership in a racial group, it becomes difficult to ascertain the salience of biraciality or multiraciality in relationship to the specific provisions and intended benefits of these Federal laws and programs. There are for sure numerous combinations of biraciality and multiraciality. What can be stated about common experiences shared by biracial or multiracial persons? . . . biracial or multiracial persons have the burden to document what distinct experiences or disadvantagement, in contrast to persons of protected single race backgrounds, they have had because of their biraciality or multiraciality before the decision to establish a multiracial or biracial category would be appropriate.

At this point, it is not clear whether a multiracial category is a racial minority category that warrants a distinct category for federal policy purposes. What is clearly emerging is that a multiracial identity is a viable identity for some Asian Americans.

Transnational Identity

The various meanings of "Asian American" presented thus far have been in relationship to other Americans, both majority and minority settlers. Two emerging meanings of Asian American, however, are in relationship to other Asians throughout the world.

First is the relationship of Asian Americans with Asians who have emigrated from Asian countries of origin and settled in other regions—for example, Vietnamese Chinese, Japanese Canadians, and Asian Indian Ugandans. What Asian Americans share with other Asians is a secondary ethnicity with their geographic and cultural origins being distinct from present birthplace and residence. They are a new group of people with ancestry in one society who migrate and exist over several generations in another society. The younger generations, however, are immigrating to the United States, creating yet another Asian American meaning. For example, the numbers of Asians with Hispanic origins may include not only children of Asian and Hispanic parents but the second- and third-generation Asian Panamanians who are establishing residence in the United States. That is, Asians of secondary ethnicity migrate to the United States and join their Asian American cousins, contributing to a new layer or tertiary ethnicity.

Second is the relationship of Asian Americans to their countries of origins. With rapid global transportation and communication, Asian Americans can travel regularly across the Pacific for leisure and business. They divide their time between the United States and Asia and fit easily in either environment. They are bilingual, bicultural, and binational. This is a little known but potentially growing population, particularly as U.S. trade in Asia increases and there is development of a sizable middle class in some Asian countries, including China and India. A transnational identity supersedes the current classification which focuses on intergroup relations within the United States.

In the case of either a multiracial identity or a transnational identity, the racial category of Asian American becomes secondary or inappropriate. If these identities become popular, they may threaten the viability of Asian American as either a racial category or an ethnic group. The probability of these two identities, however, is for now relatively infrequent.

SUMMARY AND CONCLUSION

The status and identity of various population groups are a combination of definitions by the group itself and by the larger society. In the United States, definition has been primarily by the larger society. A White majority has been distinguished from racial and ethnic mi-

norities, namely American Indians, Asian Americans, Blacks, and Hispanics. Racial categories became the proxy for minority status first
when they were used to support policies of exclusion and later when
they were used to affirm policies of inclusion.

Only in the past two decades have racial and ethnic categories been
formalized in the federal policy known as Statistical Directive 15.
Based on this policy, extensive data have been collected on the size,
proportion, household and family composition, education, employment, income, and health of these selected groups. For Asian Americans these data have been particularly voluminous as they are often
available for several subgroups as well as the total Asian population.

This wealth of data has become available just as Asian Americans
are beginning to view themselves beyond a racial category. This is not
to say that racial classification is no longer necessary or to suggest that
race is no longer a salient feature for Asian Americans. Rather, it is to
suggest that a definition by racial category is not sufficient to understanding what it means to be an Asian American. Asian Americans may
no longer be viewed solely as a racial group but also as a pan-ethnic
group which is defined beyond a majority-minority paradigm.

This shift away from a racial category and toward an ethnic identity
is also occurring among Blacks and Whites with the use of terms such
as African American and European American. What is happening is
that groups are undergoing an evolutionary process of self-identification which may not continue to be dependent on a majority/minority
status. Asian Americans have defined themselves not just by a White
majority but in relationship to other racial minorities and other Asians
throughout the world. They are in interethnic and interracial relations.
They are likely to maintain clan and regional identities as well as multiracial and transnational identities. Simultaneously, their socioeconomic status, in general, parallels that of the non-Hispanic White
population.

This evolutionary process, however, is not straightforward but cir-
cuitous, which is to say that instances of racial discrimination may
occur which can quickly reinforce group solidarity and minority group

status. Recent attention to improper campaign funds in the 1996 presidential elections coupled with restrictions on immigrant populations in immigration and welfare legislation has resurrected the image of Asian Americans as foreign and alien. Thus, while Asian Americans will continue to exhibit a multiplicity of identities in the foreseeable future, the salience of race is ever near. A racial category for Asian Americans continues to be relevant but must be complemented by other meanings of "Asian American."

NOTES

1. In 1970, the Japanese, Chinese, and Filipinos were the largest Asian American groups.

2. Seven percent of all public schools, mainly in the West, use "Filipino" as a separate racial/ethnic category in addition to the five federal categories of Directive 15 (U.S. Department of Education, 1996).

3. These are lower than the national per capita average income of $14,143.

4. Since 1970, the Bureau of the Census has allowed self-identification by only one category. Respondents who provide more than one category are reclassified into the first category listed. The National Center for Health Statistics has classified children by the mother's race since 1989.

5. On a similar note, there were more American Indians of Hispanic origin (8.44 percent) than there were Whites of Hispanic origin (5.79 percent).

BIBLIOGRAPHY

Bean, Frank D. and Marta Tienda

1987   *The Hispanic Population of the United States.* New York: Russell Sage Foundation.

Bennett, Claudette E.

1992   *The Asian and Pacific Islander Population in the United States.* March 1991 and 1990 Current Population Reports, Population Characteristics P20-459.

Bennett, Claudette E. and J. Gregory Robinson

1993   Racial Classification Issues Concerning Children in Mixed Race Households. Paper presented at the annual meeting of the American Statistical Association, January 3-5, Fort Lauderdale, Florida.

Committee on Post Office and Civil Service

1994   *Review of Federal Measurements of Race and Ethnicity; Hearings Before the Subcommittee on Census, Statistics and Postal Personnel.* House of Representatives, Serial No. 103-7. Washington, DC: U.S. Government Printing Office.

Congress of the United States

1988   July 15 letter to Dorothy Tella, Office of Management and Budget, from Augustus Hawkins, Mervyn Dynamlly, Edward Roybal, Patricia Schroeder, Ted Weiss, Matthew Martinez, Robert Garica, Don Edwards and John, Conyers, Jr.

del Pinal, Jorge

1993   Impact of Ethnic Data Needs in the United States. In Statistics Canada and the U.S. Bureau of the Census, *Challenges of Measuring an Ethnic World.* Washington, DC: U.S. Government Printing Office.

Der, Henry

1994   Statement of Henry Der, National Coalition for an Accurate Count of Asians and Pacific Islanders. In *Review of Federal Measurements of Race and Ethnicity; Hearings before the Subcommittee on Census, Statistics and Postal Personnel.* House of Representatives, Serial No. 103-7. Washington, DC: U.S. Government Printing Office.

Edmonston, Barry, Joshua Goldstein, and Juanita T. Lott, eds.

1996   *Spotlight on Heterogeneity: The Federal Standards for Racial and Ethnic Classification Summary of a Workshop.* Washington, D.C.: National Academy Press.

Edmonston, Barry and Charles Schultze, editors

1995   *Modernizing the U.S. Census.* Washington, DC: National Academy Press.

Espiritu, Yen Le

1992   *Asian American Panethnicity: Bridging Institutions and Identities.* Philadelphia: Temple University Press.

Farley, Reynolds and Walter Allen

1987   *The Color Line and the Quality of Life in America.* New York: Russell Sage Foundation.

Federal Interagency Committee on Education

1975   Report of the Ad Hoc Committee on Racial and Ethnic Definitions of the Federal Interagency Committee on Education, Washington, DC.

Fetterman, David

1988   *Excellence and Equality: A Qualitatively Different Perspective on Gifted and Talented Education.* Albany: State University of New York Press.

Gates, Henry Louis Gates, Jr.

1995   What's in a Name? Some Meanings of Blackness in Rico. In Barbara Roche and Sandra Mano, eds., *American Mosaic: Multicultural Readings in Context.* Boston and Toronto: Houghton Mifflin.

General Accounting Office

1993   *Census Reform: Early Outreach and Decisions Needed on Race and Ethnic Questions.* Washington, DC: General Accounting Office.

1992   *Federal Data Collection: Agencies' Use of Consistent Race and Ethnic Definitions.* Washington, DC: General Accounting Office.

Hacker, Andrew

1992   *Two Nations: Black and White, Separate, Hostile and Unequal.* New York: Ballantine.

Hahn, Robert

1992   The State of Federal Health Statistics on Racial and Ethnic Groups. *Journal of American Medical Association* 267, no. 2.

Harrison, Roderick and Claudette Bennett

1995   Racial and Ethnic Diversity. In Reynolds Farley, ed. *State of the Union: America in the 1990s. Volume Two: Social Trends.* New York: Russell Sage Foundation.

Hing, Bill Ong and Ronald Lee, eds.

1996   *Reframing the Immigration Debate.* Los Angeles: LEAP Asian Pacific American Public Policy Institute and UCLA Asian American Studies Center.

Hirschman, Charles

1993   How to Measure Ethnicity: An Immodest Proposal in Statistics Canada and the U.S. Bureau of the Census. In *Challenges of Measuring an Ethnic World.* Washington, DC: U.S. Government Printing Office.

Isajiw, Wsevolod

1993   Definition and Dimensions of Ethnicity: A Theoretical Framework in Statistics Canada and the U.S. Bureau of the Census. In *Challenges of Measuring an Ethnic World.* Washington, DC: U.S. Government Printing Office.

Lee, Rose Hum

1949   The Decline of Chinatowns in the United States. *American Journal of Sociology,* March.

Lesser, Jeff H.

1985-   Always Outsiders: Asians, Naturalization, and the Supreme Court.
1986   *Amerasia Journal* 12, no. 4: 83-100.

Lieberson, Stanley

1980   *A Piece of the Pie: Blacks and White Immigrants since 1880.*
Berkeley: University of California Press.

Lieberson, Stanley and Mary C. Waters

1988   *From Many Strands: Ethnic and Racial Groups in Contemporary
America.* New York: Russell Sage Foundation.

Lott, Juanita Tamayo

1989   *Knowledge and Access: A Study of Asian and Pacific American
Communities in the Washington, D.C. Metropolitan Area.* Report
commissioned by the Smithsonian Institution, Washington, DC.

Mark, Diane Mei Lin and Ginger Chih

1982   *A Place Called Chinese America.* Dubuque, IA: Kendall/Hunt.

Miyamoto, Joanne

1971   What Are You? In *Asian Women.* Asian Women, Berkeley: University of California.

Multi-racial Persons of Southern California

1988   April 14 letter to Dorothy Tella, Office of Management and Budget from Nancy G. Brown.

National Asian Pacific American Legal Consortium

1995   *1994 Audit of Violence Against Asian Pacific Americans.* Washington, DC: National Asian Pacific American Legal Consortium.

National Research Council

1978   *Counting the People in 1980: An Appraisal of Census Plans.* Washington, DC: National Academy of Sciences.

Office of Management and Budget

1995   Standards for the Classification of Federal Data on Race and Ethnicity Notice. *Federal Register* 60: 44674-44693.

1994   Hearing on Directive No. 15, Volume I: Transcript of Public Hearings, Kamehameha School, Kapalama Heights, Honolulu, Hawaii, July 13.

1978   Statistical Directive No. 15: Race and Ethnic Standards for Federal Agencies and Administrative Reporting. *Federal Register* 42: 19269-19270.

O'Hare, William P.
1992   America's Minorities—The Demographics of Diversity. *Population Bulletin* 47, no. 4.

Parsons, Carole W., ed.
1972   *America's Uncounted People.* Washington, DC: National Academy of Sciences.

Petersen, William
1983   Politics and the Measurement of Ethnicity. In William Alonzo and Paul Starr, eds., *The Politics of Numbers.* New York: Russell Sage Foundation.

Population Reference Bureau
1996   World Population Data Sheet. Washington, DC: Population Reference Bureau.

Rumbaut, Ruben and Kenji Ima
1988   *The Adaptation of Southeast Asian Refugee Youth: A Comparative Study.* Final report to the Office of Refugee Resettlement, U.S. Department of Health and Human Services.

Shinagawa, Larry Hajime and Gin Young Pang
1996   Asian American Panethnicity and Intermarriage. *Amerasia Journal* 22, no. 2: 127-152.

1996   The Impact of Immigration on the Demography of Asian Pacific Americans. In Bill Ong Hing and Ronald Lee, eds., *Reframing the Immigration Debate.* Los Angeles: LEAP Asian Pacific American Public Policy Institute and UCLA Asian American Studies Center.

Snipp, Matthew
1989   *American Indians: The First of This Land.* New York: Russell Sage Foundation.

Statistics Canada and the U.S. Bureau of the Census

   1993   *Challenges of Measuring an Ethnic World.* Washington, DC: U.S. Government Printing Office.

Takagi, Dana

   1992   *The Retreat from Race: Asian-American Admissions and Racial Politics.* New Brunswick, NJ: Rutgers University Press.

Takaki, Ronald

   1979   *Iron Cages: Race and Culture in Nineteenth-Century America.* New York: Knopf.

U.S. Bureau of the Census

   1997   Results of the 1996 Race and Ethnic Targeted Test. Population Division Working Paper No. 18.

   1996   Findings on Questions on Race and Hispanic Origin Tested in the 1996 National Content Survey. Unpublished staff working paper.

   1993a   *We, the American Asians.* Washington, DC: U.S. Bureau of the Census.

   1993b   *1990 Census of the Population: Social and Economic Characteristics for the United States.* Washington, DC: U.S. Government Printing Office.

   1992a   *Population Projections of the United States, by Age, Sex, Race, and Hispanic Origin: 1992 to 2000.* Current Population Reports P25-1092. Washington, DC: Bureau of the Census.

   1992b   *Statistical Abstract of the United States, 1992.* Washington, DC: U.S. Government Printing Office.

   1992c   *Detailed Ancestry Groups for States.* Report 1990-CP-S-1-2. Washington, DC: U.S. Government Printing Office.

   1991   *Race and Ethnic Origin, Content Determination Reports.* 1990 Census of Population and Housing, 1990 CDR-6. Washington DC: U.S. Government Printing Office.

   1933   *Fifteenth Census of the United States, 1930 Population,* vol. 2. Washington, DC: U.S. Government Printing Office.

U.S. Commission on Civil Rights

   1979   *Civil Rights Issues of Asian and Pacific Americans.* Washington, DC: U.S. Commission on Civil Rights.

1978   *Social Indicators of Equality for Minorities and Women.* Washington, DC: U.S. Commission on Civil Rights.

1973   *To Know or Not to Know: Collection and Use of Racial and Ethnic Data in Federal Assistance Programs.* Washington, DC: U.S. Government Printing Office.

U.S. Department of Education, National Center for Education Statistics

1996   *Racial and Ethnic Classifications Used by Public Schools.* Statistical Analysis Report, NCES96-092.

U.S. Department of Health, Education and Welfare

1974   *A Study of Selected Socio-Economic Characteristics of Ethnic Minorities Based on the 1970 Census.* Washington, DC: Department of Health, Education and Welfare.

U.S. Department of Labor, Bureau of Labor Statistics

1995   *A CPS Supplement for Testing Methods of Collecting Racial and Ethnic Information.* Report.

Wei, William

1993   *The Asian American Movement.* Philadelphia: Temple University Press.

Weil, Frank

1993   August 1 letter to Honorable Tom Sawyer, Chairman, Subcommittee on Census, Statistics and Postal Personnel.

White, Pamela, Jane Badets, and Viviane Renaud

1993   Measuring Ethnicity in Canadian Censuses. In Statistics Canada and the U.S. Bureau of the Census. *Challenges of Measuring an Ethnic World.* Washington, DC: U.S. Government Printing Office.

Women's Legal Defense Fund

1988   July 15 letter to Dorothy Tella, Office of Management and Budget from Claudia Withers, Brenda Smith and Nancy Kreiter.

Wong, Paul

1972   Emergence of the Asian American Movement. *Bridge Magazine* 2, no. 1.

INDEX